The History Of My Stupidity

By Dave "Beaker" McNichols

Illustrations by Michael Chau

2019

This is dedicated to my lovely wife, my funny kids, and my patient parents.

Ansie,

I hope you enjoy the read!

Your friend,

Dan

June 2023

Contents

Foreword	vii
Acknowledgements	ix
The Set Up	x
Chapter 1 Some Stupid Stuff I've Done	1
The Pull-Up Bar	2
Skateboarding Genius	4
The Doggy Door	8
❖ Stupidity Break: New Cop	11
Surround Sound	13
Milk	18
Green Carpet	22
❖ Stupidity Break: Ashtray	23
Bike Riding	24
Nard Protector	26
'72 Super Beetle	30
❖ Stupidity Break: The Mall	36
The Mailbox	38
The Green Waste Receptacle	41
Shallow Grave	44
❖ Stupidity Break: Driving Fluid	47
Backing Out Of The Driveway	50
Bob's Big Boy	53
Softball	57
❖ Stupidity Break: Uncle John	60
Golf	62
❖ Stupidity Break: Rat Trip	67
Sheet Cake	69
Iron Man	71
❖ Stupidity Break: Dude, Where's My Car?	73

Chocolate Chip Cookies	75
More Chocolate Chip Cookies	77
Aliens	80
❖ Stupidity Break: The Third Reich & Wyatt Earp	83
She's Hot	85
Elementary School	88
High School	90
❖ Stupidity Break: Piano Lessons	96
Cinco de Mayo	98
Martinez	102
I'm Dying	104
❖ Stupidity Break: Grinder Haven	106
Yogurt	107
Rental Cars	110
Driver's License	112
❖ Stupidity Break: Zip It	114
Chapter 2 My Life In Music And Stupidity	**117**
Beginning Drums	118
Beaker	121
Elvis	123
Senior Recital	125
Pictures With Presidents	129
How Does This One Go?	131
Do You Know Anything About Jazz?	133
Naked Baby	135
Fuel	136
Sliced American Cheese	138
Monopoly And Dr. Pepper	142
A Cleansing	143
Gone Fishing	145
Horsey Video	146
❖ Stupidity Break: Tacet	149

Jesus Paid It All	152
I Can't Hear	157
My First Recording Session	162
Tacos	169
Potato Salad	174
❖ Stupidity Break: Special Mic And Wayne	178
Small Sausage	184

Chapter 3   My Brother Is Stupid   186

My Brother Is Stupid	187
The Picture Window	188
Fire Extinguisher	190
Oreo Cookies Grow In The Front Yard	192
Privacy	193
"I'm Going Into The Navy"	194
"I'm Getting Out Of The Navy"	195
Birthdays	196

Chapter 4   My Stupid Brother Gets His Own Chapter   202

Immaculate Deception	203

Chapter 5   My Lovely Wife   209

Dinner	210
Sewing 101	213
Facebook	215
School Sports	216

Chapter 5   My Mother-In-Law   217

Nemo And Friends	218
I'll Pay	225
Recycling	227
Birthday Party	229

Epilogue   230

The History Of My Stupidity

Foreword

I have issues. I've lived on this planet long enough to realize that most people are stupid and, the older I get, the less patience I have with others because of their stupidity. But they are not alone. I have joined them on many occasions. Instead of just drinking and smoking while sitting in my boxers watching television, I decided to record the history of my stupidity. So I've been sitting in my boxers, watching television while eating Cheetos, typing away with two *Cheeteld* fingers on my iPad to chronicle these wonderful events (I don't drink or smoke; never have).

And as an extra-added bonus, I've included the stupidity of my brother and a few moments of brain weakness for my wife and mother-in-law. I've also included what I call *Stupidity Breaks*, where you take a break from reading about my stupidity and enjoy learning about the stupidity of others. Friends and family (those who will admit it)...please enjoy.

Acknowledgments

This book didn't start out as a book. It started with me wanting to document the stupid things I've done or that have happened to me throughout my life. In recent years I've spent a lot of time on planes and decided to make good use of my time by writing. I knew that I had a handful of stories, which would come up in conversation periodically over the years, but as I started to write, I started to remember more stories. And it grew.

I added stories that involve my stupid brother, my lovely wife, my wonderful mother-in-law, and various friends and other family. So now it's a book.

I offer my thanks to those who have aided in or witnessed my stupidity over the years, those who have offered up their own stupidity for the public to view (Darian Goddard, Jeff Cagle), and those who have relayed stories they've experienced (Uncle Bill).

I also would like to thank Michael Chau for his wonderful illustrations! In addition, and most importantly, a huge thanks to my smart, wonderful, and beautiful niece, Laurelin Varieur, who edited this and in the process taught me a lot of stuff.

The Set Up

Most, and possibly all, who read this know me to some extent. Some through music, some through work, some through just plain friendship. And then there's family, including my stupid brother. Here's a little set up about me for a frame of reference, since I don't post every bowel movement on Facebook for all to enjoy:

I was born and raised in Upland, CA, to my loving parents Bev and Hugh who adopted me at birth. My brother was eight years old when I arrived, and he was just growing into his stupidity at the time. I grew up playing sports and started playing drums at 13. When I was about 18, I decided I wanted to play music for a living, but after struggling to break into the LA studio scene, I realized that I didn't want to play bars and weddings. So I set my sights on getting a *real job*. Through a family connection, I landed in the transportation/supply chain business and have made that my career.

I've been able to continue playing music both professionally and for fun for the past 40 years while progressing through my career. My music friends say to me, "You have a *real job*?" And my supply chain associates say to me, "You play music?"

I've been married to the love of my life, Cindy, for 34 years and definitely married up. We have three wonderful children. Kristin, our oldest, is 32. She is autistic and is the happiest kid on the planet. Kristin loves doing jigsaw puzzles, listening to music, watching home movies and *Wheel of Fortune* (her brother was actually on the show), and visiting Disneyland. She moved out at 24 into a full-time home for those with special needs, and couldn't be happier. It was the most difficult decision we ever made — and frightening — but turned out to be the best thing for her and us. I actually believe Kristin is the normal one in the family.

Jason, 28, is an actor, director, stand-up comedian, and musician living his dream. Most likely, all of his funny is from me. He is a graduate of The Second City Conservatory in Hollywood, where he has performed and directed. He has done several national commercials (Apple, Slim Jim, Six Flags, Virgin America), TV shows (*Malcolm in the Middle, The Winner, Rake, Dr. Ken*), and feature films (*Camp Fred, Camp Takota, Visions*).

He currently works for Disney.

Sara is our youngest at 26. She's actually pretty smart, which I don't think she got from me. She has a bachelor's degree in political science, and at one point she had a goal of becoming The President of the United States. We'll see. The pay is above average but there's a little stress that comes with the job. She currently works for Disney, alongside her brother, and loves it. She loves spending her spare time with friends and family.

After expertly raising our children, and being Kristin's full-time caregiver for 24 years, Cindy is living her dream by working at Disney. She started working in the attraction "Innoventions" (formerly the "Carousel of Progress"), then transferred to New Orleans/Critter Country to work the attractions "Winnie the Pooh", "Splash Mountain", and "Pirates of the Caribbean." She now works in the entertainment division and trains new cast members. If you ask nicely, she can introduce you to Mickey or Pooh. Wouldn't you love to meet Pooh?

On to stupidity...

Dave, Kristin, Cindy, Sara, Jason

Chapter 1

Some Stupid Stuff I've Done

The Pull-Up Bar

I was 10 years old and decided I needed to start working out. Figured I wasn't buff enough. Not sure what prompted this. Maybe the ladies. So I found a pull-up bar in the house (most likely belonging to my stupid brother). This is the type of contraption that you place between a doorjamb and twist to tighten. I was probably about four feet tall at the time, so I placed the bar in my bedroom doorway at about 5'10". Since the bar was out of reach as I stood below, I placed a small metal stool directly beneath it. Hop up on the stool, do about two or three pull ups, and buffness ensued.

After I go to bed that night, my dear old dad decides to come and kiss me goodnight. He walks from the kitchen into the dark hallway and turns right towards my bedroom. As he attempts to enter my doorway, he simultaneously strikes his head on the bar and his little toe on the stool.

After numerous sounds and unknown words exit his

mouth, I see blood streaming out of the crease in his forehead while he hops around on one leg holding his toe in utter pain.

I don't believe I ever received the good-night kiss that night, and the pull-up bar and stool were gone when I woke up.

Skateboarding Genius

When I was growing up in the 60's and 70's in Southern California, we played outside every day after school, unlike today where you hardly see kids doing this. They're inside playing a video game, on social media, or watching TV. I'm not sure which one is better because we tended to get into trouble trying to find something to do.

When I was about 10 years old, my neighborhood friend Joey and I were riding skateboards. Up and down the sidewalk, in and out of driveways — mild stuff. Eventually, we ended up at Joey's house and were sitting on our boards, pushing ourselves around his garage in a circular pattern.

These were the early days of skateboarding and the equipment wasn't the best. The wheels were hard and the bearings didn't allow for a lot of fast, easy movement. Because of this, we kept putting oil in our bearings to make the wheels turn smoother and faster. At 10, I was not a mechanical genius, so I used way too much oil, too often. So did Joey. Soon we had a trail of oil on our little circular runway. This made it fun because we literally slid around the track.

Like I said, I wasn't a mechanical genius, just a normal 10-year-old genius, but I knew that if a little oil made our track fast and fun, then a lot of oil would be even better. My cohort agreed. We take the remaining oil from my dad's oilcan and some oil we found in Joey's garage and pour it onto the garage floor, covering our track. There's about an eighth of an inch of oil spread across our garage speedway.

We push ourselves around the track for a while until our fun gets old. We walk out through the open garage door with our boards in our hands and, as we look back into the garage, we can see that it is a mess. Oil is everywhere. We know we can't just leave it for Joey's dad to come home and discover. His mom is in the kitchen, just inside the side garage door, but we don't think of asking her for help. We might get in trouble if we do that. I have what I think is a great idea: Light it on fire and it will burn itself clean. Joey thinks this is a great idea, too.

He finds a matchbook, lights one, and throws it onto our oily track. Instantly, the whole track explodes with flames reaching the ceiling. We are panic-stricken and can't believe our eyes. Almost simultaneously, his mom opens the door between the kitchen and garage, most likely to see what kind of trouble we are causing.

Her premonition is right. She slams the door on the 15-foot flames and comes running out the front door onto the driveway, probably thinking her house is on fire. By this time, the flames have died down. No more fuel; it had burned up. I was right, the genius that I am.

The Doggy Door

While my wife, Cindy, and I were visiting her Grandma Carter one day, Grandma mentioned that she needed a doggy door installed in her mobile home. She wanted to give outdoor access to Tiny, her mean little prized Chihuahua. Grandma Carter was a wonderful woman with a very interesting past. She grew up in the south and trekked west when she was about 18, with her mom, by hopping on a freight train. Somewhere along the trip west they hooked up with the circus. Her mom was the tattooed woman. Grandma Carter's real name was Willie Mae, but her friends called her Bill. She had an interesting family too, including a cousin named Scoot. I've used all this info and more to bag my wife's family, when needed. I come from a line of pastors and educators. She comes from hobos and carnies.

So I tell Grandma Carter that I can put her doggy door in. I've put a few in at various homes we've lived in, so no big deal — and I would love to help her out. I survey the wall where she wants the door placed; looks easy. All you do is use the template that comes with the doggy door, cut the hole, and install it. The wall of this mobile home is about as thick as cardboard, so I don't see any issues. About a week later I show up with the new doggy door, a power drill, a power saw, and a couple other tools. I use the template to mark the wall for the cut, then drill a couple pilot holes to allow the saw blade to get a start. Then I start sawing through the wall, which is like a knife in soft butter, until I reach the electrical wires, which I never dreamed would be there. Shock, sparks, amazement! It was pretty cool. Scares the crap out of me and Grandma Carter. I stand back to assess the damage, and that's when I notice a plug to the right of the impending hole, and one to the left. Both at the same height as the middle of the proposed new doggy door. Genius.

I stand there scratching my head, staring at a wire cut into two pieces and half the electrical off in the home. Fortunately, the mobile home park had a handyman who came to the rescue by running new wires between the plugs and completing the job I started. The moral of the story: Dogs can be a pain in the ass.

STUPIDITY BREAK

New Cop

My friend Darian used to be a cop in Florida. He was real young when he became a cop, and he himself can't believe they issued him a gun and sent him out there on the streets to keep the peace. On one of his first days of training he was working traffic. His training officer was an old codger, on the force for years, who had seen it all and was close to retirement. He smoked a cigar nonstop.

Darian is driving and the old guy is riding shotgun, literally. Darian sees a lady driving a car that breaks some traffic law so he lights her up.

She's driving an old station wagon with the fake wood paneling down the side, similar to the car in the first vacation movie with Chevy Chase. She starts to pull over and he's following close behind her. The old codger is just smoking his cigar, watching it go down.

Darian is attempting to change something with the lights while pulling over to the side of the road. This is the first time he's done this, and he runs right into the back of the lady's car. Without removing the cigar from his mouth, the old cop says, "It's all you, cowboy."

Surround Sound

Soon after moving into the home we live in now, we purchased our first flat screen TV and had it professionally mounted with all the electrical fished through the wall. The work was done by one of my closest friends, Felix. He also mounted the front surround sound speakers. Felix is a high-end finish carpenter and his work is always first class. I can't afford him, but since we're friends he helps us out here and there. I was assisting him with this job and decided that it would be too much to ask him to mount the rear speakers as well. I figured I would do it later. He had to come up with a special way to mount the left and right speakers and he painted the brackets he made flat black to match the speakers. They looked great. When he was done, he had me touch up the wall paint around the speakers and TV mount. The wall color was Navajo White. Like any typical dunce, I tried to use a roller, which sprayed Navajo White all over the freshly black-painted brackets. Nice. I'll never hear the end of that one.

After enjoying our new TV with surround sound for a while, I wasn't sure if I was missing anything by not having the rear speakers in place. We only had the sub and the front speakers. One Saturday, I decide to tackle the rear speaker mount job. After some breakfast, my wife heads out shopping with the kids in tow. I survey the job at hand and determine where I want to mount the speakers: on the ceiling just behind where the couch sits, one left and one right. That was the easy part. The hard part would be running the wires from the TV through the wall to the attic, across the attic, then down to each speaker.

I grab a ladder and mark the spots where I want the wires to come down from the attic, then punch holes at each mark. Next, I straighten out two wire hangers and push them up through the holes so I will have a way to know where the holes are when I get up into the attic. Then I run a wire fish up the wall behind the TV into the attic. I move the ladder to the attic opening in the laundry room and go up. In my younger days I was tall and skinny. These days, not so much on the skinny side, so traversing through the attic all in the pursuit of perfect sound wasn't the best idea. Additionally, it was summer. It was about 85 degrees outside and warming. Heat rises.

I get up into the attic with the wire in my pocket and a flashlight. The attic in our home is not built like a loft. It has the trusses that support the roof and insulation. The design of our ceilings has a lofted area in some rooms and lower flat ceilings in others. In the family room we have a lofted ceiling and a couple skylights. I work my way over one truss at a time, pulling my leg over then stepping on the rail below. Then another, and another. About 10 feet over from the attic entry on the way to the area above the family room is where several trusses meet from different angles, and there is a square entry you have to crawl through to get to the other side, around the skylights. I stick my arms through and then pull my body through. It was very tight.

Just getting this far is a huge task. I'm sweating like crazy and breathing harder and harder. It must have been over 100 degrees up there. I had also started to cough from breathing in the insulation. I don't realize this will be a problem until I get up there. I start to think it might be a good idea to go back down and get a mask. My coughing worsens, almost to the point of gagging, and I start to overheat. I know I need air and start to panic and get claustrophobic as I maneuver back through the small opening, but I make it out and back down the ladder. I take a few minutes to collect myself while cooling off and drinking water. Then I search the garage for a mouth and nose mask, but I can't find any. I take a trip to Lowe's to get some, then back to the coal mine. I wasn't smart enough to give up.

I put my mask on and head back into the attic. Up and over one truss and another, then another, through the small opening, around the skylights, and I make it. I tie the wires to the hangers, then get out of there. Back on solid ground, I pull the wires through and hook them up to the speakers. I was spent! Red-faced, disheveled, and still hacking a little from the insulation, but I had triumphed! Cindy gets home around this time and sees how I look and asks me what the heck I've been doing. I explain to her exactly what you just read. That's when she tells me how dumb I am and that no one was home and I could have passed out up there and no one would have known.

I throw in an action movie DVD, turn on the TV and surround sound, and sit back to hear the amazing difference in audio. I can barely hear anything coming from the rear speakers. An ambient sound here and there, very faint. Underwhelming.

Milk

One of the first jobs I held was working at a drive-thru dairy on Arrow Highway in Upland, CA. I started at Arrow Dairy when I was 16. The owner was a friend of our family. His name was Chuck. We had two lanes for customers to drive through and order various dairy products and assorted other groceries. I waited on customers, stocked, and completed inventory daily. Chuck and his family lived on the other side of a wall, which was on the north side of the inner drive-thru lane. Chuck had a doorbell installed which could be signaled from the dairy in case he was needed for something. Periodically, a customer would request something special or a vendor would arrive needing Chuck's assistance, so we would ring the bell.

I loved working there because I had all the snack items you could dream of at my fingertips and at a reduced rate. I would have the 6-pack of little chocolate donuts with milk, or chips and a soda, or my favorite...vanilla Zingers with milk. Yum. Then for lunch or dinner I would hit EZ Out Burger right down the street. We also sold gas at the dairy, with two gas pumps out front. Typically once a month, a customer would forget to remove the hose from their tank and would drive off, tearing it out of the pump. Lots of fun.

One day, a regular customer comes in — an older single woman. She never seemed happy, and I remember her always requesting a gallon of the newest-dated milk available. This particular day was early in my dairy career. She rolls up in the inner drive-thru lane at a very busy time in the evening. I have cars in line in both lanes. She rolls down her window and hands me a gallon milk container with about a third of the milk left. She tells me that the milk is spoiled and she wants a new gallon to replace it. I look at the date stamped on the container, which has passed. I'm not sure what to do at this point, so I ring the bell for Chuck. As usual, Chuck steps out of his home, about 40 feet from the dairy, and looks over the wall. With customers all around me waiting, I yell loudly, "We have some spoiled milk!" Nice work, dunce. Chuck is waving his arms for me not to speak anymore as he makes his way over to me to handle it. This became a moment of learning for me.

I wasn't a complete dunce, though. A year later, Chuck sold the dairy and I continued to work for the new owner. One day, they had scheduled two of us to work, expecting it to be very busy, and it wasn't. There was hardly anything to do. The shelves were stocked, the reefer had been cleaned, and inventory taken. We stared at each other. I was looking for other things to do and remembered how dirty the bathroom was. I don't ever remember it being clean. The job of cleaning it had never been assigned to any of us that I knew of. I tell my co-worker to mind the store because I'm going to clean the bathroom.

I gather up all the cleaning supplies I can find and go to work. Seems like six inches of dust and grime on everything. I scrub the walls, the floor, the toilet, the sink, the pipes, the door, and the window. It is spotless when I get done. I clean myself up, put the cleaning supplies away, and go back to work in the dairy. A couple hours later the owner arrives to check on things. He comes into the dairy and with a very stern and direct delivery asks, "Who cleaned the bathroom?" I think for a second that I might be in trouble for leaving the store to clean it. I slowly raise my hand, thinking I might now get fired or yelled at. He excitedly points at me and says, "50 cents per hour raise for you! Thanks for taking the initiative to clean it. It looks spotless!" Nice, I learned something again.

Green Carpet

I was five years old when we moved into the house that my parents still live in. It was 1965. The carpet color de jour was Tall Fescue Green. So I do what any smart five-year-old would do. I put the sprinkler in the living room and turn on the water. I figure that green carpet needs watering like a green yard. Apparently it didn't.

STUPIDITY BREAK

Ashtray

Darian's training officer used to use the mounted shotgun as his ashtray. He would drive around, patrolling the city, sucking on that cigar and would tap the ashes into one of the barrels of the shotgun. One day, a hot ember from the ashes ignites the ammo in the gun and blows a round right through the roof of the patrol car.

Bike Riding

When I was 12 years old, I convinced my mom to let me ride my bike all the way to McDonald's for lunch on a Saturday. It was two miles away, up on Foothill Boulevard in Upland. I would ride east to 2nd Avenue, then take it north all the way there. Same order every time: two Big Macs, a large fry, and either a coke or two milks. I would eat in the dining area, then ride back home. Since I made it there and back without dying, my mom let me do it periodically.

I decided to venture out to a different fast food restaurant: Mi Taco. I'm not sure how I discovered this place, but I didn't get the Mexican food; I got the burger. It was fantastic. So were the fries. Mi Taco was about a mile from our house, straight west on 7th Street. So one Saturday I hit up my mom again to let me go there and she agrees. I ride to Mi Taco and order two cheeseburgers and large fries. This time I decide to take it home and eat it, so I pedal as fast as I can so I will still have warm food when I get home. I get something to drink, then sit down at the kitchen table. I open the bag to find a taco and a burrito. Nice. Good job. I get back on my bike, pissed, ride back to Mi Taco and get the correct order, then ride back home.

This event changed my life. From that day on, I have checked every fast food order BEFORE I leave the restaurant.

Nard Protector

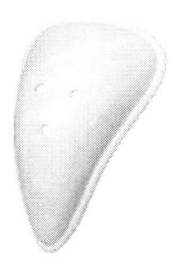

I played baseball while growing up. Loved the game and Johnny Bench was my hero. I played catcher in Little League because of him. When I tried out for Little League, they sent me out to left field to shag fly balls. The fly balls started coming, and I caught every one. They kept coming, more towards left center field, then towards center field, and I kept snagging them. I wondered how many I had to catch to prove my skills. More came towards right center, then towards right field. Finally, I hear the coach yelling. I stop and look at him. He tells me to stop catching everyone's fly balls. I look around and there are 10 other fielders. And that's why they made me a catcher.

Required gear for a catcher includes shin guards, a chest protector, a helmet, a mask, a catcher's glove, and a cup…otherwise known as a *nard protector*. Not a drinking cup, but a specially-designed plastic device which covers your wee-wee and cha-chas. This cup is to be worn inside a jock strap, which keeps it in place. The team provided all the gear including a cup, but I used my own. For some reason, I wasn't keen on the jock strap. It was kind of a weird contraption, and I wasn't real sure how it was supposed to be worn. Do I wear underpants and the jock strap? That seemed like too much. But wearing only the jock seemed like going commando and I didn't like that feeling, either.

Since I didn't wear the jock strap, I would place the cup in my baseball pants on the outside of my briefs. This worked until I ran, and then the cup would slide down my pant leg. I would then call time, run into the dugout, reach down my pant leg and pull the cup back in place. Such an idiot.

One Saturday, I decide to use the team's cup instead of mine, so I leave my cup on my bed and go to the ball field. That particular Saturday, my dad had to work and I'm not sure where my mom was. My brother was at home. Being the starting catcher, something I had worked toward for a couple of years, I had started and played all six games of the season. This was game seven. We are out in the field and a batter hits a foul ball real high between home and first base. I throw the mask and start running to catch it, never taking my eyes off the ball.

Just before the ball falls into my glove, the first baseman and I collide. I hit the ground landing awkwardly on my left arm. It's killing me. I have never felt pain like this before. They help me get off the field and into the dugout and the second string catcher takes over. The pain does not subside, so they call my home to see if one of my parents can come and pick me up and take me to a doctor. My brother was home and took the call. They tell him that I have been injured and need to be picked up and taken to a doctor. He says he'll be right there. He goes into our room to get his shoes, sees my cup on the bed and is horrified, thinking I must have taken a baseball right in the nards. Not the case. I broke my arm, out for the season. And I never made the Major Leagues, either.

As a side note, when I was growing up I had a friend who signed up for Pop Warner football. He goes to the first orientation meeting with his dad and they give him a list of things to buy before the first practice: pads, cleats, jock strap, cup. A nard-protection cup. My friend gives the list to his mom and asks if she can go to a sporting goods store to buy these things for him. She agrees. Apparently the list described which pads, so she buys those. She waits on the cleats so he can be there to try them on, and she gets him a jock strap. Last thing on the list: *cup*. She buys him a drinking cup and decides to put his name on it so it won't get mixed up with anyone else's *cup*. His name is Tag.

'72 Super Beetle

One of my first cars was a 1972 Volkswagen Super Beetle. I wish I still had it. It was a great car. I drove it from 1977-1984. I installed an 8-track player and beefed up speakers. It was bitchin. Here is a list of the 10 albums I carried on 8-track in my car: Chicago's albums *I* (*Chicago Transit Authority*), *V, VI, VII, VIII, X*, stacked in order, then *Foreigner (self-titled first album), Boston (self-titled first album), Toto (self-titled first album)*, and Toto's *Hydra*. The tunes were great in my car.

One rainy day, I'm cruising from a friend's house in Rancho Cucamonga to visit a girl friend — not my girlfriend, but a close friend who was a girl — Teri, in Upland. In 1977, the city of Rancho Cucamonga was not fully developed. Flood control infrastructure was not in place. The flood control consisted of asphalt or concrete north-south roads with three-foot rock walls on each side, which kept the water in the road as it traveled south from the mountains. Apparently everyone but me knew you shouldn't attempt to travel on these roads during heavy rain. And heavy rain was what we were having. It had been raining hard all day long.

I'm driving west on 8th Street in my Super Beetle, with the little windshield wipers working as fast as they can, and I can barely see out my fogged-up front window. I approach Hellman Avenue, which is a four-way stop. As I stop at the stop sign I can see some water moving south, but it looks shallow enough to drive through. I take off headed west, where the road descends, basically because Hellman was built and used as a heavy wash street. By design, it's lower than the east-west streets to keep the water moving south. All of a sudden, I'm moving south with the current. It is so strong that it turns my car around and I don't have enough power to fight it. This is not good. Just 50 yards south is a huge wash that comes from the foot of the mountains, collecting water from all the north-south streets and running diagonally across Hellman. And the current is taking me there.

The wash could have three feet of water or more in it moving at a fast pace like a small river. That scared the crap out of me.

I am able to quickly turn into the driveway of a home on the east side of the street to get out of the current. Then what to do? I figure I should go north on Hellman, back to 8th, and back to safety. I find enough room to turn the car around so I won't have to back out. I drive back out onto Hellman in first gear, revving it hard, and head north towards 8th. The RPMs are maxed out. As I approach 8th and start to turn and ascend up, the engine dies and the current turns me back around headed south again towards the wash. Now I notice that the car is starting to fill up with water. It's wet up to my shoes, covering the floorboard. No time to worry about that; I'm headed towards the wash. I try to start the car and it won't start. I put it into second gear, push the clutch in, turn the key off, then on, then drop the clutch to start it. It works, and just in time to turn into the same driveway again to safety.

I sit there pondering my next move. I don't like the idea of spending the night in my car in this driveway, wet up to my ankles. What to do? I turn the car around again facing towards the street and try driving north one more time. I make it about half way back to 8th and the engine dies again. *Screw it*, I think, *I'm going through the wash*. The current turns me around again and I'm headed south. I put it in neutral and pick up speed. Just before the wash, I drop the clutch into second gear again. The car starts and I take off as fast as I can through the wash, driving over a couple of huge rocks in the process, but I make it out and up to a clear road. As I'm driving away from the wash, I notice how much water is in the car. My feet are literally under water.

    I drive straight to Teri's house, park, and turn the car off. She opens the door, takes one look at me and says, "You look like you've seen a ghost." I tell Teri and her family what has just happened to me, and they are thankful that I lived through it. Teri's stepdad was a mechanic, so he goes outside to check my car. It won't start at this point and since the engine had gotten wet, it would require a tune up to get it running again. We tow it to my house and push it into the garage.

    The next day I try to start it again, thinking it might have dried out, but no go. I purchase the parts to do a tune up and get to work. I replace the plugs, points, and change the oil and filter.

I also lube the wheels and joints, and take off the shifter plate and grease it up. All done, turn the key, and nothing. I check with my dad and he thinks the battery might be dead and suggests we push start it. We push it out of the driveway and into the street. Then I get in the driver's seat, turn the key on, push the clutch in, and put it in second gear. I drop the clutch. Nothing. We try it again. Nothing.

Then my dad figures we aren't going fast enough, so he decides to push me with his car, a 1973 Ford LTD. This car was built like a tank. It had a huge bumper with two vertical bumper guards.

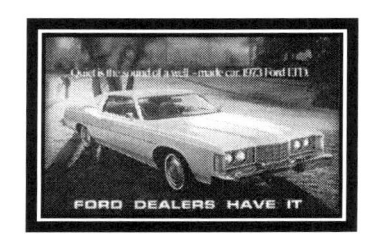

He pulls the LTD behind me and tells me he'll push and yell when to drop the clutch. I have it in second gear, key on, clutch in, brake off, and he starts pushing. We get up to about 20 mph when he yells. I drop the clutch and the car stops dead in its tracks. The LTD slams into the back of my car, destroying my engine cover and ruining some of the engine parts. This is not good. I'm pissed and blaming my dad.

We are sunk now and call a tow truck to tow it to a local shop. We find a shop that specializes in Volkswagens, owned by an old German guy. We figure he knows Volkswagens since he's German. He checks it out and has it fixed in a couple days. We go to pick it up and he starts telling me I don't know how to take care of a car properly. He accuses me of covering the engine with plastic to keep it dry, and that the plastic has melted into parts of the engine. I'm not sure what he's talking about. I had never put plastic on it. Maybe the owner before me did. He asks me if I had removed the shift plate at some point. I tell him I had removed it after the water incident to put grease on it, and then reinstalled it. Apparently I put it on backwards, so when I thought it was in second it was really in reverse. That's why the dropped clutch move didn't work and that's why the car stopped on a dime each time I dropped the clutch.

He gives me a look like I'm some young American dumbass teenager. He was right. He was much older than me so I'm pretty sure he's dead now.

STUPIDITY BREAK

The Mall

When my son Jason was in high school, going to the mall became the thing to do. He and his friends would go and just goof around, probably to look for girls and to basically just be stupid like teenagers do. It was typical for him to be joined by Tyler and Joey. We knew both boys and their parents and believed they were good kids. We were stupid. So were they. Fortunately, they've all lived and have grown up without major disasters.

This one particular weekday evening while my wife and I are hanging out in our family room with our daughter Sara, Jason asks if he can go to the mall. At the time, Jason was about 16; Sara 14. I ask if his homework is done. It is not, but he says he'll finish it before he leaves.

I remotely believe him, since we had homework history that wasn't pleasant. I ask who is going, and he says a couple names we don't know. Doesn't seem like a good idea. Weeknight, school the next day, no business at the mall except to wreak havoc, and joined by boys we don't know. Denied.

I tell Jason that I'm not comfortable with him going with friends we don't know and state that it makes more sense to stay home and do homework and chill. He leaves the room, shoulders slumped, dejected. He returns about two minutes later with a lift in his step, holding his cell phone claiming that Tyler has just called and he can go to the mall. "Hand me your phone," I say.

He uncomfortably brings me his phone. I look up the recent calls...none from the previous couple hours. "You haven't received any calls," I say, as I look at him with disgust. Again he leaves the room, shoulders slumped, dejected. Sara is amazed at what a genius I am. For a moment, I *was* a genius.

The Mailbox

We live in a very nice, quiet community on a cul-de-sac. The mailboxes are grouped together in fours on a structure consisting of a vertical 4x8 buried in cement about eight inches below the surface, with 2x6 strips mounted horizontally, which the mailboxes are attached to. These structures are strategically placed every three houses or so, in the grass parking areas just inside the curb. We just happen to have one in front of our house. One day, I notice that the 4x8 protruding from the ground has deteriorated due to 10 years of weather and sprinkler love. It is leaning, near death. I decide to spend my Saturday as the savior of the shared mailboxes for our neighbors and us.

First thing Saturday morning, I hit Lowe's for supplies, then return home to tackle the job. First order of business is to remove the existing structure. A worm could have done that by leaning on it. I, too, am able to accomplish this. Next, break up the existing concrete footing. I take the first swing with my sledge, striking the footing dead square, and all of the energy and inertia I've created reverberates throughout my body, like Wylie E. Coyote in the old Hanna Barbera cartoons. I check to see how much damage I've done. None, except to my body and soul. As the outside temperature increases to the low 90s, I keep swinging at it to no avail, sweating and cursing. At this point, my neighbor Doug steps outside and witnesses my struggle. Doug is a man's man, a heavy equipment mechanic and, unlike me, he is used to manual labor. He does the smart thing and sends his twenty-something strong and in-shape son over immediately to help. We are now taking turns swinging the sledge at the resistant concrete footing. No breaks; no cracks.

  The three of us are now standing there in disbelief, staring at the footing when my beautiful wife drives up, returning from the grocery store. She steps out of the car, walks over to us and, probably thinking I should have been done by now since she's an expert on installing grouped mailboxes, she not-so-innocently asks what we're doing. I believe my response was one that would endear any husband to his wife...something like... "We're having a picnic, what does it look like? We're trying to replace the 4x4 footing so we can remount the mailboxes, but we can't get the old footing out." As I stand there in frustration with my blood boiling from the idea that I could even be questioned about my plan, my wife offers a solution. "Why don't you just put a new footing next to the old one?" The three men think quietly, considering this option. I distinctly remember my next statement to my wife: "Why don't you go inside and sew something?" I should have expected a sledge strike to the head at that point, but fortunately my wife has patience and restraint.

As soon as my wife shuts the front door, we all agree that her idea is genius. We dig a hole next to the stubborn concrete mass, pour a new footing and move on with our lives.

The moral of the story: buy a house with a mail slot in the door.

The Green Waste Receptacle

It was a fall Sunday afternoon. I was the only one home, sitting in my chair watching football. The day before, I had raked all the leaves in the back yard and moved them into piles, but had not moved them into the green waste receptacle yet. I figured I better do it before it got dark because I was traveling the next morning and would be gone all week. I wanted to get the leaves out for trash day on Tuesday.

I go to the side yard and roll the receptacle to the back yard. These receptacles are typical in most communities these days. They're issued by the trash company. In our area, you get a black one for trash, blue for recyclables, and green for garden and yard waste. They're about four feet high, and two feet square. I start at the first mound of leaves and load them into the container. I then decide to move the container to the next mound, but I don't close the lid. I lean the container back and take a step forward to roll it to the next area. When I tilt the container back, the lip of the lid drops to the ground, and I step on it, pulling the whole container to the ground and me into it, slamming my left bicep into the top in the process. This all happened in a split second. Gravity won. There I am lying head in, feet out, face full of leaves, with excruciating pain in my left arm. It felt like someone had struck my arm with a sledgehammer.

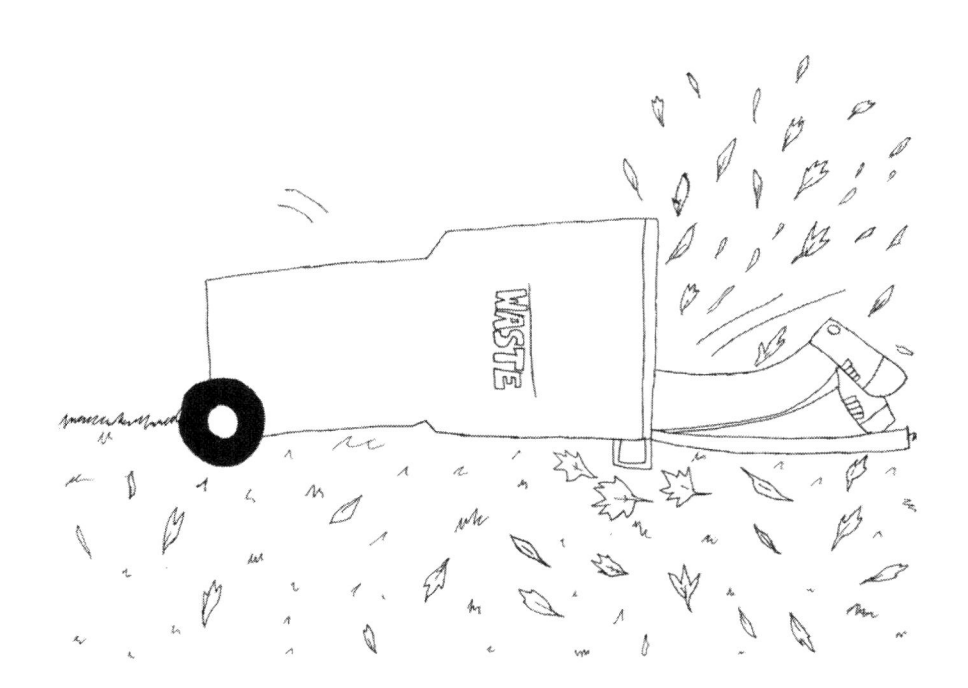

Concerned that someone may have witnessed all of this, I shimmy my way back out of the container and sheepishly look around while dealing with the pain. No witnesses. I take a break for a few minutes to let the pain subside, and then I finish the job. I go back into the house and take my place back in my chair watching football. Soon after, Cindy gets home. I tell her what happened and show her the huge purple bruise covering my arm. Her reaction? She starts laughing as she pictures me head down in an upright container, legs and feet sticking out, and is bummed she didn't get a picture or video. That's not how I landed, but that's how she wanted it to be. Nice compassion.

Shallow Grave

One Saturday when I was about 17 years old, a friend and I planned to go play basketball with some friends, so he picked me up in the late morning. I left my keys at home since I wasn't driving, and normally one of my parents was home so I wouldn't need a house key. We took off and returned a few hours later. We used the back door of our home as the main entrance, so I walked down the side of the house, across the patio, and up the steps to the back door. It was locked. I rang the doorbell, but no one answered. I checked the garage and my parents' car was gone. My parents weren't home.

This is the point when I realize how bad I have to go to the bathroom...#2. I need to get in the house. I try the front door, but it's locked. I check all the windows, but all are locked. I think I might be able to jimmy the back door lock, so I get a screwdriver from the garage and try to pry the jam open and get to the lock. At the same time, I'm squeezing my cheeks together to keep from unloading one in my pants. I try everything on that doorjamb but nothing works. All I did was ruin it.

With my parents apparently gone for the day and no way

for me to contact them, I know I'm not going to get into the house in time. I can't squeeze it much longer, so I scope out a place to deliver. This was before my parents put a pool in, so they had a grass back yard with bushes and plants along the walls. There is one area that looks promising: a palm tree with a bush on either side. Looks good to me. I drop my load right next to the palm tree, and then bury the goods in a shallow grave. I think I used leaves to clean up with. Very resourceful. I was now ready to live in the wild.

I take a seat on the patio and wait for my parents to come home. When they arrive, my dad notices the destroyed back door jam and asks me what happened. I explain that I had left my keys in the house and was just trying to break in. I don't tell him how I just helped fertilize the back yard. All is good.

About a week later, we notice that our little dog Puddin' is sick, acting droopy and not eating. My mom tells me that she's taking her to the veterinarian. She returns a couple hours later and tells me that Pudin has worms. I'm puzzled. I've never heard of that before, so I ask how a dog gets worms. My mom's response: "The vet said that sometimes dogs eat their own feces."

"Oh," I say. My mom says that we have to do a better job of picking it up in the back yard. "Yes, we do," I agree.

I never told my parents the truth, but I did tell this story to my wife. Then one day while we were visiting my parents, 20 years after this event, my wife drops that bomb. "Remember that time when you..."

STUPIDITY BREAK

Driving Fluid

One thing I have not done well is teach my kids how to take care of a car.

They know how to drive and how to put gas in, but that's about the extent of it. I've never been much of a car guy. I love cars, but I don't know how to work on them and have no interest in learning. That's what professional auto mechanics are for. I can put fluids in, change a battery, and have been known to replace a radiator hose a few times, but only out of necessity. I grew up with friends who were totally into working on cars, taking engines apart and beefing them up. Seemed to me like they would put a lot of time and money into their engines, then when it was time to show off they would go fast and sound loud for about a minute, then blow something and head back to the garage.

Though I could tell he was not really paying attention, I showed Jason a few things as he grew up. Sara? Not so much.

I would routinely check the oil in their cars to make sure they didn't burn up their engines, like my stupid brother did to his '63 Volkswagen Bug...dumbass.

So one day when Jason is about 20 years old, he calls me to let me know his car isn't running well. I ask him what the symptoms are. He says it drives fine, then has no power. I'm trying to figure out what it might be and I hear someone talking in the background with Jason. It's one of his friends. Jason tells me that his friend says it needs *driving fluid*. "Driving Fluid?" I confirm. "What is driving fluid?" I ask. Jason doesn't know. "Does he mean transmission fluid or oil?" Then I hear his friend say, "Driving fluid." I'm not a mechanic, and not a genius, but I pretty much know it doesn't need *driving fluid*. Seemed like it might be a fuel pump problem.

Jason was living in Hollywood at this time, about an hour away from us, so I had him call AAA to tow it to a local shop.

I call the owner of the shop who turns out to be a great guy. He's been running his shop for many years. I explain that my son is 20, an actor, living in Hollywood and he doesn't know much, if anything, about cars and that we are an hour away.

He says he will check it out and call me back. I tell him what Jason's friend said, that it needs *driving fluid*. "Driving fluid," he repeats. "Hmmm. I think I'm all out of that. In fact, I've never heard of it." We have a good laugh.

The next morning, he calls to advise that it was the fuel injector. He replaces it and we are good to go. No driving fluid needed. Unless you call unleaded gasoline driving fluid, in which case his friend was correct. You do need it.

Backing Out Of The Driveway

Leaving for work one morning, I followed my typical routine. Wake up, take shower, put clothes on, eat breakfast, brush teeth, put shoes on, grab keys and roll. Waking up for me is a relative term. I generally don't wake up fully for an hour or so. My wife learned on day one of our marriage not to try to have a conversation with me until the cobwebs have cleared and the monkeys in my brain start pedaling. Unless there's an emergency, this takes a little time.

My 2002 Toyota RAV4 was parked in our driveway facing the garage. A nice, quiet, warm and sunny day. I walked down our driveway, which is sloped downward from the garage towards the street, and slid into the driver's seat. I started the car, put it in reverse, and disengaged the parking brake. Nothing fun and exciting about this day so far, but that was about to change. A split second after my hand left the brake handle, I realized I had left my cell phone in the house, so I quickly opened the car door and stepped out.

We now have an emergency. I'm standing between the open door and the car as it starts driving itself down the driveway, backwards, curving slightly. I am now fully awake. I swiftly maneuver my overweight frame with the car, back peddling and side shifting like an NFL player in a training camp drill, attempting to avoid death or severe injury while I devise a plan to stop the vehicle, yelling, "Oh shit, oh shit..." continuously.

Fortunately, there are no cars parked in front of our house because the RAV4 has now made a semicircle turn and is headed towards the group of mailboxes in its path, and I'm still in between the door and car running sideways, facing epic failure. I finally decide it's time to save the day and I jump into the driver's seat and step on the brakes. I wish I had this on video because I'm sure it looked awesome. No damage, no injury. I step out of the car (after putting it in park and setting the brake) first to see if any neighbors witnessed this historic event. No one in sight. I retrieve my cell phone from the house and continue another typical day.

Bob's Big Boy

One of my all-time favorite restaurants is Bob's Big Boy.

I used to eat there often in my younger days. There are still a number of Big Boy restaurants open for business, but I've only found one that still tastes like the original, and that's the one in Toluca Lake, CA. This was one of the originals and is the oldest still in business. It's run very well, open 24 hours, service is great, and it tastes like the old days. Bob Hope used to frequently have lunch there, since he lived about a hundred yards away, and the Beatles ate there on the same trip that they played the Hollywood Bowl. I eat there often too, but my picture isn't on the wall.

Recently, my wife and I had dinner there with my cousin Tami. Tami drove in from her home in Ventura to meet us for dinner and to see my son's show at The Second City in Hollywood. We were seated at a booth and gave our order. When the food arrived, I grabbed the ketchup bottle and lightly shook it back and forth to mix up the ketchup. You know how the ingredients of ketchup separate when idle, so you have to mix them up a little. Apparently, this can cause a chemical reaction, which I was unaware of, but was about to experience.

As I have the bottle in my right hand, lightly shaking, the top blows off and ketchup flies out of the bottle. At first, I realize that I have it all over my shirt, then my cousin Tami looks over to my right and says, "Oh my." I look over and see a beautiful young girl in a white and light green frilly lace dress, covered in ketchup. She is at least six feet away in another booth with her mom and a friend. She has ketchup all over her right side, on her dress, her arm, her neck, her face, and her hair. I cannot believe the horror I am witnessing.

Tami jumps up, grabs some napkins and water and asks the girl if she can help clean her, to which the girl agrees. She and her group are somewhat laughing and wondering how this happened. I apologize over and over and offer to pay for her dress. She tells me it's not necessary, that she bought it for $10 at Ross for one event, which she just went to. Tami is doing a great job of cleaning her up, dabbing napkins in water and wiping the affected spots and cleaning her skin. The girl's mom inquires, "You must be a nurse."

"No," says Tami, "I'm a teacher."

Meanwhile, my wife is helping by loudly asking me how I did this. "Did you check the cap?"

"Cindy, not now," I whisper.

"How hard did you shake it? You know you have to hold the cap if you're going to shake it?" she says.

"Cindy, stop it!" I exclaim. She isn't helping. I offer to pay for their meal but the server acknowledges that this has happened before, a chemical reaction. It wasn't my fault. Bob's paid for their meal. I was exonerated.

A picture from another
visit to Bob's with
family

L-R: Jason, Avery (Tami's son), Cindy, Sara, Dave, Tami

Softball

Just after high school, I joined an intramural softball league. I loved playing baseball while growing up, and this was a way to keep fit and have fun while continuing with the sport. In this league you fielded 10 players: pitcher, catcher, four infielders, four outfielders. You had to have a minimum of seven to play a game; any less would require a forfeit. I remember one game when we had all 10 of our players, but our opponent only had six. They offered not to forfeit, stating that they could cover the field and pitching with six if we could supply a catcher. We agreed, thinking we'd kick their ass.

The first time they went out to the field they had a pitcher, a first baseman, a second baseman, a right fielder, a center fielder, and one guy positioned to cover short, third base, and left field. One guy for the whole left side of the field. We thought this was too easy. We would just hit everything to that side of the field and there was no way he could cover it. What we didn't know was that he used to be the backup infielder for the Cincinnati Reds in the 1970s, behind guys like Davey Concepcion and Joe Morgan. We got nothing passed him and they beat us miserably. But that's not what I wanted to write about.

With the goal of trying to impress her, I invite Teri to one of my games. Being the amazing softball player that I was, I figure she will witness greatness, which will make her want to be my girlfriend, not just a girl friend. My brain must be small. She comes to one of my games and watches. It's not like today where everyone has a smart phone and they can be at the game, but not watching it since their face is buried in the phone. Back then there weren't any distractions. She has 100% focus on the game.

I get multiple hits, steal a few bases, and score several runs. There are a bunch of plays where I have to slide to beat throws, and slide into home to score a run. I also make some great fielding plays, diving to make catches and to stop grounders and throw someone out. After the game, I meet up with Teri in the stands, dirt all over the uniform I'm wearing like a soldier who has just fought and won a battle, and I ask her how she liked the game. I'm waiting for her to say how amazing it was and how great I did.

Instead... "What happened? You kept falling down out there." Apparently, she didn't know how baseball — or softball — works. I was disappointed.

Here's a pic of me during softball times.
L-R: My stupid brother, Great Aunt Fern, Thelma Skillin, Beaker

STUPIDITY BREAK

Uncle John

When I was 13 years old, our family went on vacation from Southern California to Washington state to visit my mom's brother and family: Uncle John, Aunt Dianne, and my cousins Brad, Jeff, and Tami. My brother was in the Navy at this point so it was just my dad, mom, and me. I was getting more into skateboarding at this time and I built a small wood ramp, which I could ride up on and do some tricks. I would ride on it daily, so I was bummed that it was too large to bring on vacation. When we got to my aunt and uncle's house, I had fun hanging out with family, especially my cousins. We would go out to their back yard and ride my skateboard around their patio. My Uncle John has always been fearless and up for a challenge, especially with sports, so he rode my skateboard around, too. He was about 40 years old at the time.

I told him about the skateboard ramp I had built and asked if he could build something like that. Of course he could, and he did. He immediately got to work pulling lumber and tools out of his garage and in a very short amount of time I had a ramp.

It was made out of 3/4-inch plywood, supported by 2x4s. It was about six feet wide and four feet deep and sloped from the ground up to about a foot high. He placed it on the grass in the back yard, just off the patio so I could ride off the patio, onto the ramp, do a trick, and then come back down to the patio. It worked great! I was really excited.

After I rode on it a few times, my uncle said he wanted to try. He puts one foot on my board and starts pushing with the other foot to gain speed. As soon as he reaches the ramp and tries to go up it, the board shoots out from under his feet and up the ramp into the sky. He falls backwards abruptly onto the concrete patio, breaking the fall with his upper back, shoulder and head. Gravity won. Fortunately Uncle John was ok, but Aunt Dianne was not pleased with him trying to act like a teenager.

Golf

A buddy of mine, Tim Schrader, sent me a text inviting me to play golf with him and another friend named Drake. I was in. It was a Friday and I took the day off. We had beautiful weather, clear, sunny and warm. We played Sierra Lakes Golf Club in Fontana, one of my favorite courses in the area. We had a foursome, but I don't remember who the fourth was. We teed off at about 9:30 a.m. Things were a little slow out of the gate but opened up after a couple holes. Tim and Drake can really drive the ball a long way, mostly in the fairway. I'm not a long hitter, but I'm usually pretty straight.

We get to the third hole, a par 5, and all of us hit our drives. Four balls in the fairway. I typically cannot reach the green in two on a par 5 (except hole 13 at Richmond Country Club one time in 1998. Driver, 4 wood to 6 feet, made the eagle putt. Not that I remember it well). Tim and Drake both hit it long enough to reach. We pull up to my shot and I hit my second to about 70 yards off the green. The group in front of us is on the green, putting. We move up to Tim's ball and check the yardage. He might be able to reach, but it would be a stretch. Tim asks me what I think. I tell him that from the yardage it looks like he can't reach, but he might roll it up close to the green. I suggest that he hits to keep the flow of the game moving. One of golf's biggest problems is slow play. Anything that players can do to help speed it up without pushing anyone or being unsafe is welcomed by most.

Tim pulls a club, gets set and hits it. He drills it, headed just left of the flag. The group in front of us is still on the green, but Tim's ball lands about 20 yards short of the green and rolls up to about five yards away. The rest of us hit our approach shots and start heading towards the green. This is when we see one of the players in the group ahead of us standing on the green, arms crossed, I'm-a-bad-ass stance, looking at us. *Hmmm*, I think. *Does he think we were trying to hit into them?* As we approach the green, he starts to walk away but keeps staring us down with this *I'm pissed* look. He and his group move to the next tee and we arrive at the green. As we're putting, I look over and see him standing on the next tee box, arms crossed, staring at us.

He's a thirty-something white guy, about six feet tall, in

shape, wearing Dickies shorts, tall white socks, tennis shoes, and a ratty shirt. Might not even have had a collar. He's all flexed out, veins nearly popping out of his neck. Tim notices the guy and makes sure I see that he's staring us down. I say to Tim, "I've got this."

Tim says, "You sure?"

"Yeah, I got it," I say. Tim has a look of concern on his face. We drive up to the next tee and now two guys are staring at us.

Me: How you guys doin?

Mr. Dickies: Not so good since you hit into us.

Me: We didn't hit into you. That ball landed 20 yards short of the green.

Mr. Dickies: It looked a lot closer than that.

Me: Dude, there's no way that ball was going to hit anyone. We're just trying to speed up the pace of play.

At this point, the dude is all flexed up at me, like he wants to fight. Juvenile.

Me: Why are you all flexed up at me?

Mr. Dickies: I'm not.

Me: Is this your first time playing golf?

Mr. Dickies: Yeah, it is. (*sarcastically*)

Me: Good, now you know how it works. We're not trying to hit you, just trying to keep the pace of play going.

Mr. Dickies mumbles something unintelligible. Not a stretch for him.

Me: Why don't you get in your white truck and drive back to Corona?

(*Let me clarify the meaning of this: Typically, the epitome of a Southern California douche bag is one who wears Dickies shorts, long white socks, drives a jacked-up white truck, and lives in either Corona or Riverside.*)

And with that, he put his little tail between his legs, wet his pants, and moved on to the next hole, never to be heard from again.

I'm an overweight, fifty-something white guy who has never been in a fight, and I pick one with a roided-out Dickies douche bag. Pretty smart.

Tim Schrader, Beaker, Drake Kelley

Must have been striped shirt day.
And look at me! It looks like I'm
hiding a 50 pound sack of manure
under my shirt.

STUPIDITY BREAK

Rat Trip

Speaking of golf, after one of my golf outings I placed my clubs in the garage like always. A few weeks later I went to retrieve them for another round and discovered huge holes in each of the pockets and quickly realized that a varmint had eaten through them, ruining a good bag. I had inadvertently left some food in one of the pockets. I didn't achieve the physique shown in the picture on the previous page by forgoing food while on the golf course, so I must have had some cookies or cheese crackers in there. He chewed through some golf balls too, hoping the center would be scrumptious. I'm sure the nasty varmint had a nice little meal. That was until he went for dessert and somehow opened a bottle of ibuprofen, one that contained 50 pills when purchased and of which I had only taken 4.

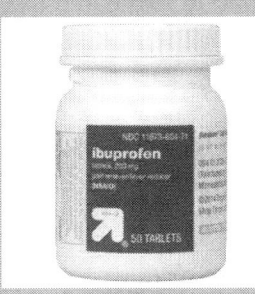

He managed to empty it into his little gut, happily enjoying the sugar coating of 46 pills at 200 mg each. I wish I had video of the trip he went on before he expired. We did smell him for a couple days after his little party in my golf bag but never found the remains.

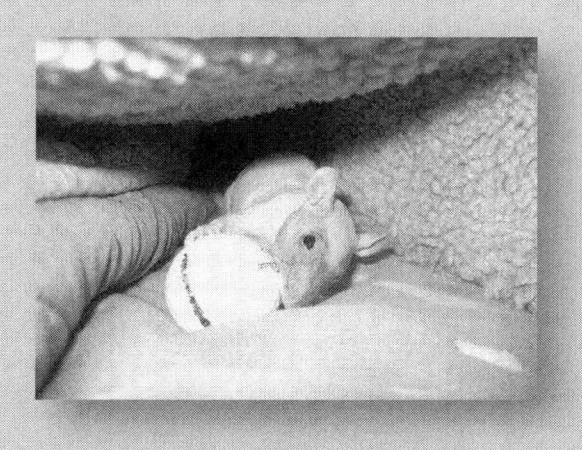

Sheet Cake

My mom is a great cook and baker. Her baking skills were influenced by her mom and family when she was growing up, then by my dad, who grew up in a bakery run by his parents. When I was about 12 years old, my mom was asked to make a sheet cake for a church function we were to attend. She made it in a 10x13 glass baking dish.

As we are getting into the car, my mom puts the dish on the floorboard behind the driver's seat and makes sure to tell me not to step in it. I think she says that about three times. I say I won't and I sit behind her on the passenger's side of the car. The drive to church is about 1.5 miles and takes about five minutes — plenty of time for me to forget what she said. So as soon as my dad stops the car at church, I proceed to step directly into the cake. I was barefoot. Fortunately, my mom had covered it in Saran Wrap. It was still edible, if you didn't mind the size 9 left footprint right in the middle.

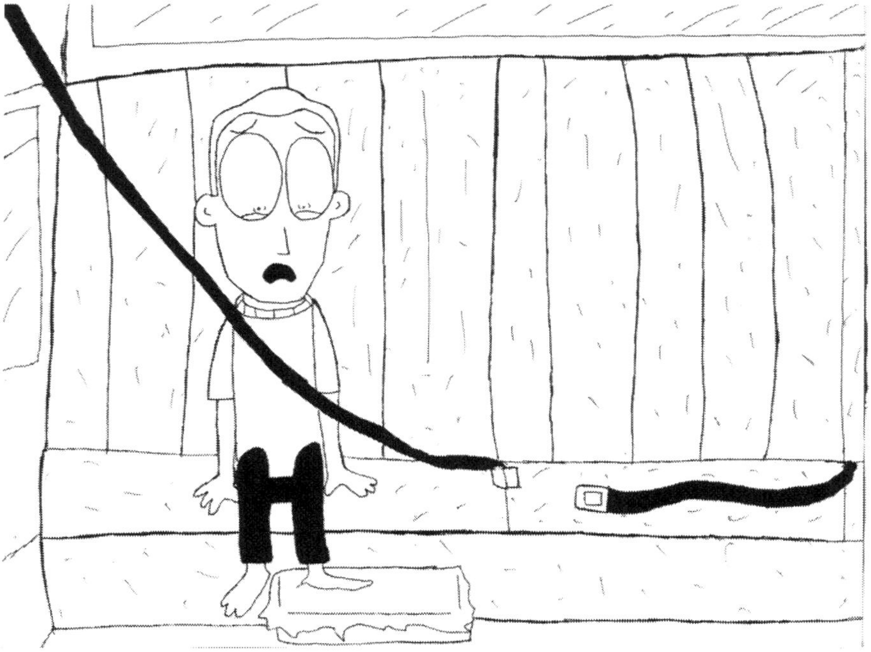

Iron Man

Just before a business trip to Dallas in 2010, I purchased a new polo shirt. A very nice one in a darker blue color and suitable for business-casual use. The first morning of the trip I'm getting my clothes ready for the day and find that the new shirt is wrinkled, so I decide to iron it. I get the hotel iron out of the closet along with the ironing board, plug in the iron and set it on high. This is what you do with an iron. Get it as hot as you can so it works properly, right?

Well, apparently a hot iron and rayon don't get along too well. I base this assumption on the fact that I have a perfect iron imprint on my dark blue rayon business-casual polo shirt. Not in an inconspicuous place. Right in the gut area. I still wore it that day because I didn't have enough other options for the week. I wore it proudly and was duly named "Iron Man," not to be confused with the comic book character.

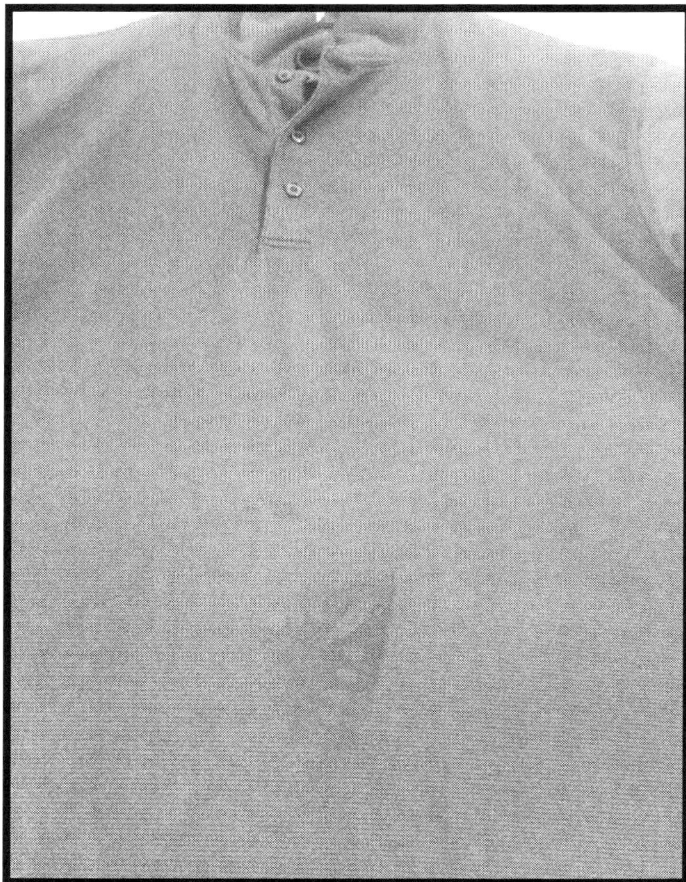

STUPIDITY BREAK

Dude, Where's My Car?

One of my good friends and counterparts is Jeff. He's a great guy and great at his job as an area General Manager in the supply chain field. At one time, he was based in Reading, PA and managed the northeastern part of the United States. His job required a lot of travel and much of it in the air. Jeff mainly flew out of Philadelphia, but once in a while he would fly out of Baltimore if the rates were lower, schedule was better, or weather caused Philly to shut down.

One time he books a round trip out of Philly, but weather shuts down the airport. He checks Baltimore and it's fine, so he quickly changes his outbound flight and drives the extra 50 miles to Baltimore/Washington International Thurgood Marshall Airport. (What, they couldn't put Thurgood's middle name in there, too?)

At the end of the week, he gets on the return flight, lands, and takes the parking bus to his regular parking spot...in Philadelphia.

It was just like the scene in *Planes, Trains, and Automobiles* when Steve Martin is dropped off by the rental car bus, then finds his assigned car space empty and turns around to find the bus long gone. Jeff's car was in Baltimore. He never changed the return leg.

Jeff had to walk back to the bus stop, take a bus back to the terminal, then take a rental car bus to rent a car and drive to Baltimore to retrieve his car.

Jeff Cagle and Me

Chocolate Chip Cookies

I love chocolate chip cookies. My mom used to make Toll House cookies when I was growing up, and I loved them. One day, around 10 years old, I decide I'm old enough to make them myself and convince my mom as such. She helps me find all the ingredients in the kitchen and shows me the recipe on the bag of Nestle chocolate chips. I tell her I can handle it from here.

Here's the original Nestle Chocolate Chip Cookie recipe from 1939:

> **Combine flour, baking soda and salt in a small bowl; set aside. Combine butter, sugars, and vanilla extract in a large bowl; beat until creamy. Beat in eggs. Gradually add flour mixture, blending well. Stir in Nestle Semi-Sweet Real Chocolate Morsels and the chopped nuts. Preheat oven to 375 degrees F. Drop rounded teaspoonfuls onto ungreased cookie sheet. Bake at 375 degrees for 8-10 minutes.**

I read this and my young brain cannot understand why you need to dirty two bowls. Why not just mix everything in one bowl then whip it up? Sounds good to me. I proceed to measure the ingredients and place them in one large bowl, knowing that I am saving work and won't have to wash two bowls when I am done.

Something goes wrong. I end up with one large bowl of a liquidy substance, which cannot be formed into rounded teaspoonfuls. It is only suitable to go down the garbage disposal. I've not since made cookies. Fortunately, I married well and my wife makes the best chocolate chip cookies in the land.

More Chocolate Chip Cookies

My friends and work associates have always known my love of cookies. One time, I was on the phone in my office catching up with an old friend whom I had worked with many years before. After asking me how I was doing, he asked if I still had cookies in my top right desk drawer...and the answer was yes.

During the "Iron Man" business trip to Dallas I was involved in a training session with several of my counterparts and a few site managers who report to me. Just before lunch, our leadership team moved to a conference room to join a conference call. Soon after, lunch was delivered by Panera Bread, and they brought our sandwiches into the room. After we were done with lunch, my boss, Rick Bowman, left the room and returned shortly with chocolate chip cookies. He knew I would be looking for them.

The conference call continues. I reach for the cookies so I can have a couple and pass them around the table. There are six of us and about a dozen mid-sized cookies. The chances of getting more than one cookie weren't good unless you got in early, and that's what I was attempting to do. The cookies are in a large plastic cup with a lid on it. I attempt to remove the lid quietly while we are on the call, but the lid won't come off easily. Rick is motioning for me to be quiet. I try again and make even more noise without success. The whole table is shushing me now so I put the cup down and wait for the call to end.

Finally it's over and we hang up. I immediately reach for the cup and again attempt to remove the cap, making a huge amount of noise, but it still won't come off. I can't believe it. It is a plain, simple, clear plastic disposable drinking cup with a plastic lid. The whole group is laughing at me. I make one final attempt, grabbing both sides of the lid and pulling with all my might, muscles flexing, and face red. Our project manager, Joy Martin, snaps a picture at this very moment. That's when I realize that the lid had been taped securely to the cup with very strong, clear, packaging tape. It is taped so well that you can't even tell. The culprits were two of my site managers, Sara Corona and Phil Leto. Lovely. They had entered the room immediately after the call just to witness my pain and suffering.

We used a knife to cut the lid off and finally enjoy the cookies. Fun for all at my expense.

This pic is out of focus. Call it an action pic. It's the only one we have of the actual event.

Aliens

The house I grew up in has three bedrooms. For many years, my brother and I shared the middle bedroom and we used the front bedroom as a den. We had twin beds with shelves mounted on the wall above the headboards. Apparently this is where you put things that will fall off during an earthquake. My stupid brother placed an old fire extinguisher on his shelf, which he had found at the beach. It was full of sand and was pretty heavy. One of his prized possessions. During an earthquake it fell and struck him in the head. Idiot.

After my brother joined the Navy, and departed for that far-off land named Port Hueneme in Southern California, the room was all mine. One early morning, around 0400, I am awakened by a sound I have never heard before. It is a low hum, a droning sound that seems to get louder the longer it goes. And it isn't stopping. At the same time, the walls of the house are vibrating. I can hear my parents talking, although I can't hear what they are saying. Then my dad goes down the hall towards the front door of the house to investigate. At this point I'm scared to death, and I'm thinking only one thing: ALIENS! Aliens must have landed a spacecraft on our roof and they are exiting the craft and coming to take us away. I yell at my dad to stop: "Don't go out there! They landed on the roof!!" My mom tells me to calm down. I pick up the home phone and dial 911. The operator answers and asks what my emergency is. "Aliens have landed on our roof," I say with complete fear and angst in my voice. She says they will send an officer, so I hang up.

    I run towards the front door to see what my dad is doing outside. He looks around the front of the house, and then comes back inside. The whole house is humming and vibrating. My mom walks into the front bathroom, jiggles the toilet handle, and the humming stops. The drone and vibration end. Apparently the flapper was not sealed tightly, allowing air to seep into the old metal pipes, which caused them to vibrate.

    I called 911 one more time and told them to disregard my prior call. I'm sure they laughed, thinking I was on LSD. I wasn't. I was 12 years old and stupid.

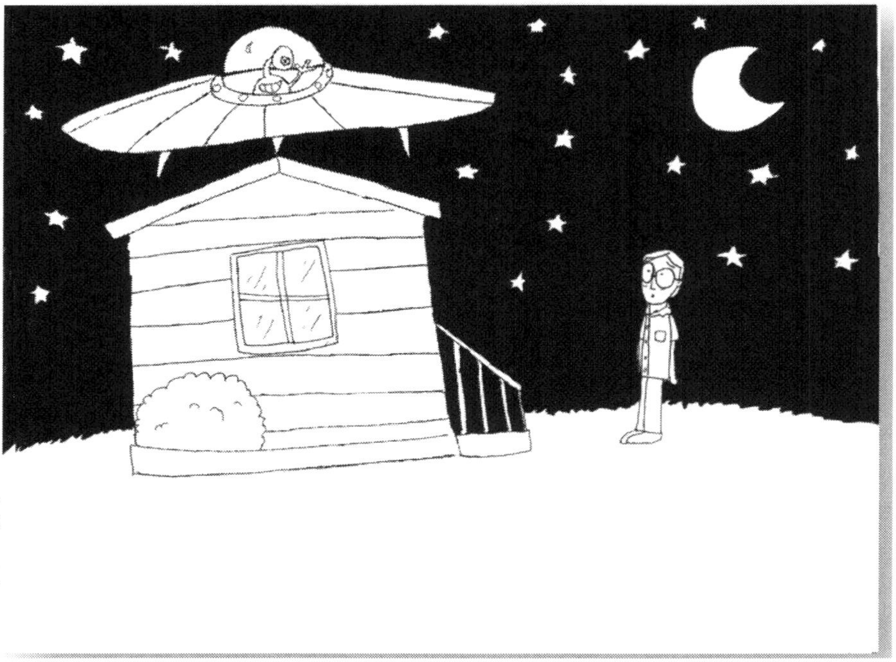

STUPIDITY BREAK

The Third Reich & Wyatt Earp

My wife's Uncle Bill used to teach high school U.S. History. One day, while teaching a senior class about Nazi Germany he shows a short film of Hitler addressing the Nazi party. During the film one of the students raises her hand, then gets out of her chair and comes up to Bill claiming that there is something wrong with the audio, and she can't understand what he is saying. Bill explains that Hitler was speaking in German. Apparently she didn't realize there were languages other than Spanish and English.

On another occasion, Bill issued an assignment to the senior class to write a paper on a person of interest from U.S. History. The students had to advise Bill whom they had chosen, then complete their research and write the paper. One student selected Wyatt Earp.

These were the days before computers, so instead of researching your paper on Wikipedia, you had to complete research using books from a library, including an encyclopedia. (Note the similarity in name between *Wikipedia* and *Encyclopedia*.)

On report day, the student who selected Wyatt Earp informs Bill that she couldn't locate any information on her subject, and therefore has no report to turn in. Bill is puzzled. He asks the student what she used for her research and she answers, "An encyclopedia, but he wasn't in there." Bill asks, "How did you spell his last name?" "U-r-p," she responds.

She's Hot

When I was a freshman in high school I tried out for the basketball team. I made the frosh-soph squad. We practiced in the main gym after school, sharing half the court with the varsity team. It was a full-court gym with a wood floor and it had extra baskets, which were lowered down from the ceiling for practice. This enabled six partial half courts for various shooting and drills. On each side of the court were grand stands containing tiered seating.

Sometimes during practice this one hot chick would walk from one end of the court to the other in front of the grand stands. It looked like she worked for the sports department since she was always carrying papers and headed to the office. All I knew was that she had short hair, was normally wearing a short skirt, and she was hot.

One afternoon we're warming up for practice. The varsity team is on the east side of the court and the frosh-soph team is on the west side. I'm shooting baskets on one of the side courts facing the north grand stand and here comes the hot chick, walking from the east entrance and heading towards the west side of the gym into the sports offices. She's wearing a short skirt and heels along with a short-sleeved top. I'm dribbling the ball...uh...hummm... with my eyes glued on her (like the coyote on the roadrunner) and all of the sudden I see in my peripheral vision two guys from the varsity team standing next to me on my right. "Do you like that? Do you want to meet her?" I turn and see that this huge guy is talking to me. He must have been about 6'6", 270. How do I know that? Because it was Anthony Munoz, the Hall of Fame offensive tackle from the Cincinnati Bengals and USC. We went to high school together.

    I say no to wanting to meet the girl. Anthony and his teammate don't seem to hear me because Anthony says, "Oh, come on, you want to meet her." Then he and the other guy physically remove me from the ground, as I fight recklessly with my six-foot, 125-pound, 24-inch waist frame (haven't seen that body in a while), and they carry me over to said hotty. They introduce me to her, the coach's daughter, and make sure to say that I wanted to meet her. I'm sure she was thrilled to meet a punk, pimple-faced geek.

Anthony Munoz

Chaffey High School
Year Book Photo

Elementary School

I attended Citrus Elementary School in Upland, CA. When I reached the fourth grade I started walking to and from school. We lived about half a mile from the school with just one busy street to cross: San Antonio Avenue. It was pretty safe since it was a four-way stop. One day I start taking a short cut, walking north on San Antonio before crossing at 7th Street, then jaywalking across San Antonio in the middle of traffic like a dumbass. Probably saved about 20 steps and maybe 15 seconds. A neighbor and friend of my mom's (known as a busy body) sees me do this one day and immediately calls my mom to notify her. This was the first time I started to believe my mom was omnipresent. How did she know I didn't cross at 7th?

My knack for finding time-saving shortcuts didn't help the fact that I seemed to have issues remembering to use the bathroom, which would cause me to routinely wet my pants on the walk home. This did create a problem for me. These were the days when the teachers would pin your homework to your sweater. Why did they do this? Because they knew if they handed it to an eight-year-old boy he would lose it before he left the school. So I would remove my sweater (with the homework pinned to it) and tie it around my waist to prevent embarrassment the rest of the way home. The homework would absorb the wetness and would then become unusable. At least I didn't have to use the old my-dog-ate-my-homework excuse.

One achievement I'm very proud of is the fact that I was the fastest runner at Citrus Elementary for one day in the fourth grade. On this day, I crafted some colorful words to a whole group of kids on the field during recess, which triggered them to chase me, threatening certain death, or worse. I ran as fast as lightning and didn't stop until the bell rang, and I lived.

High School

Like for many kids, especially boys, school wasn't fun for me except for music classes and band. Fortunately, my high school offered a percussion class, so I signed up. On the first day of class all of the students had to audition by playing from a rudiment book. You started at the beginning and played each piece, which became progressively harder. Based on how far you got through the book, your placement was determined in the class. I was able to play the whole book and became a teacher's aide, helping other students learn the rudiments of drumming. I did this for all four years of high school along with three other guys. We had a blast and basically had the run of the music building for four years.

The band director knew that he needed us, with 35+ students in fourth period all at different levels of playing and reading music. There's no way he could do it alone. As aids, we split up and each of us took a number of practice rooms, which we would oversee during the class and help our fellow students as they worked through practicing and learning to read music. I excelled in this class and got straight A's all four years. The only other subject I got straight A's in was math. Other than that, it was usually D's, barely passing.

In my senior year I had five classes. English was first period, second was math, third was history, fourth was band, and fifth was science. During the second half of the school year, my English teacher assigned a senior project, which was a choice of three things:

1. Write a paper on any subject, minimum X amount of pages.
2. Write and perform a short play in class.
3. Create a short video about a certain subject, documentary style.

I chose the video and grouped up with a couple classmates. Our subject: skateboarding. It was 1978 and skating had become the rage. The three of us were skaters and frequently visited the hot spots in the area, so this project was going to be easy.

We rented a Super 8 video camera from a local camera shop, bought tape and hit the road. When we told our teacher about the documentary project, she wrote us permission slips to miss first period so we could shoot off campus. During the first day of shooting, we realized that we needed more than 50 minutes. We decided to *amend* the permission slip to excuse us from first through fourth period. This would take us through lunch, then we could arrive in time for fifth period at about 12:30. Great plan.

We traveled all over the Inland Empire hitting all the skater hot spots: Baldy pipeline, a 10-foot diameter cement pipe at the base of San Antonio Dam, which made a great half pipe; empty reservoirs in Alta Loma; and empty pools wherever we could find them. Everything was by word of mouth. No cell phones, texting, or social media in 1978. We would hear about a new hot spot from a friend and head there to check it out. Most of the time we got lucky and happened upon some of the greatest skateboarders in history, carving it out, including Stacy Peralta and Tony Alva.

You would think that we would do this for a day or two and have enough footage to build our 10-20 minute piece. But no, we were dumbass high school students. We did this for three weeks straight, filming during first through fourth periods and *most* of the time returning for fifth period. Sometime during the fourth week, a woman in the attendance office notices I have zero attendance showing for second, third, and fourth periods for three solid weeks. She calls my house and speaks to my mom. Uh-oh. She asks if I have been missing school for any certain reason. My mom advises her that I have left for school every day during those three weeks and should have been at school. She then starts calling my teachers. My first period teacher explains that I had permission to miss her class only to work on the project. She is unable to reach my second and third period teachers but reaches the band director. She asks if I have been in his fourth period class for the past three weeks and he says yes. She inquires as to why this wasn't reported properly in the attendance records and he says there must have been a mistake and he is emphatic that I have been there every day and that I am a teacher's aid.

This leads her to believe that I must have been at second and third period as well, so the whole thing is cleared up. You wonder how I know this detail. My mom tells me that the attendance office has called and inquired of my whereabouts for the past three weeks. I play it off like they have made an error. I'm sure it was very believable. At that moment I figure I'd better start going to classes again. The next day the band director pulls me aside during fourth period and tells me about the call he got from the attendance office and that he covered for me. He explains how much he needs me in his class and basically tells me to straighten up. I am free and clear...until the mid-term grades come out. An A in band, B in English, followed by other letters which look like Ds and Fs.

My parents immediately took my car away and grounded me until I produced a diploma. I had about two months to get my act together. I did it. I passed all my classes and graduated on time. On the last day of high school, after learning that I had passed and achieved the right to graduate, my parents gave me the keys to my '72 Super Beetle back. I jumped in the car to drive to my last day of high school with a pen in my back pocket, which tore a hole in the driver's seat that had nice new leather upholstery completed a couple months prior. I'm still trying to figure out what I needed a pen for.

STUPIDITY BREAK

Piano Lessons

By the time I was seven years old my mom and dad had already seen the signs of my interest in music. I had figured out how to build a drum set with pots and pans for toms, trashcans upside down for floor toms, and pan lids hanging from shelves as cymbals. So my parents decided to start some proper musical education and signed me up for piano lessons. As you can see from the picture, my first lesson was March 4, 1968 with this sweet looking old lady.

On the occasion of my second piano lesson this woman asks me if I play any other instruments, which is when I tell her that I want to be a drummer. Then, while waving her right index finger at this young, impressionable boy (me), she says, "You need to learn the piano because it is a *real* musical instrument. Playing the drums will never take you anywhere."

Shortly thereafter I told my mom that I was done with piano lessons, thanks to this narrow-minded bitty. I'm still playing drums, going on 46 years, and being a drummer has taken me around the world and connected me with wonderful people.

Cinco de Mayo

I was born and raised in Upland, CA, which is 45 miles east of Los Angeles and about 130 miles north of the Mexican border. The racial makeup of the area when I grew up was about 45% white, 45% Hispanic, and 10% other. Although there was a heavy Mexican cultural influence, it didn't interest me. I wasn't really a fan of Mexican food, other than Americanized tacos (extra cheese please). No disrespect intended.

When I got to high school it was time to select a foreign language, which I would be required to study for three years. The thought here was that you would be fluent in this chosen language by the time you graduated and would be able to apply that knowledge and skill towards your chosen occupation. What? My chosen occupation at the time was sitting on a couch eating Cheetos and watching cartoons.

The choices were Spanish, French, and German. It seemed as if all my friends were going to take Spanish. *Hmmm. I wonder why... I thought. Could it be that they knew they needed to be fluent in Spanish to live and work in a community where close to 50% of the population is Hispanic and maybe half of those don't speak English? Nah...they're crazy, I'm taking French.* "Un French class for me."

Three years of in-depth education of a beautiful language and I can honestly say that I can count to ten and order cheese. "Un, deux, trois, quatre, cinq, six, sept, huit, neuf, dix, fromage." And of course..."Parlez-vous Français?"

This knowledge truly helped me as I got into the workforce and started managing people, mostly Hispanic. One time while preparing to draft a work schedule, I asked one of my coworkers, "When is Cinco de Mayo?" I knew it was a Mexican holiday. About what? I had no idea. When did it occur? Again, no idea. The response from my coworker: "It's the fifth of May."

"Oh," I said. "Every year?"

"Yes," he responded. "Cinco de Mayo means the fifth of May." Light bulb goes on in my head. Maybe I should have taken Spanish. Interesting side note, Cinco de Mayo is an annual celebration commemorating the Mexican Army's unlikely victory over French forces at the Battle of Puebla on May 5, 1862. So it could have been Cinquieme de Mai.

There was the one time though, when my education of the French language was useful. I was in San Francisco on business. An associate, Gary, and I were staying downtown at The Hotel Mark Twain. It's a very old building with a very small elevator. Neither Gary nor I are what you would call *petite*. We enter the tiny elevator to head towards our rooms and as the doors are closing, two individuals quickly jump in, a man and a woman. Fortunately they are very small people. Both are thin and around five feet tall, and appear to be foreign vacationers.

They can't reach the panel to select their floor number because I am blocking it with nowhere to move, so I ask what floor they want. They look puzzled and say something in a foreign language, one that I recognized. I point to the panel and say, "un, deux, trois...?"

They respond, "quatre," while gleaming with total excitement. I press four for them, six for Gary and me. Now my two new French friends are speaking a mile a minute to me in French, and looking at me like I am Jesus or Napoleon.

I just smiled and laughed, not understanding one word they were saying. Gary was shaking his head in amazement. We reached the fourth floor and they continued to sing my praises in French (I think) and look up at me like I was their savior. I shook their hands as they exited and said, "Merci." My French vocabulary had been exhausted. Fortunately they weren't staying on the twentieth floor.

Martinez

I played baseball as a kid, then transitioned to intramural softball later in my teens. When I was about 19 I joined the men's softball team at my church. We had games every Thursday night at De Anza Park on Euclid Avenue in Ontario. The games were generally around 6:00 p.m. so I would leave my house a little after 5:00 to get down there early and warm up. I would jump in my '72 Super Beetle and head south on Euclid with complete disregard for any speed limit. One Thursday I get pulled over for speeding, near H Street just south of my old high school. It's motorcycle Officer Martinez. He has the typical motorcycle cop look: standard issue helmet, aviator sunglasses, mustache, and attitude.

He cites me for 47 in a 25 at 5:17 p.m. I'm not guessing on that; I remember. This was not my first speeding violation. I sign it and take off for my game.

The following Thursday I head out from home at about 5:10 p.m. for a 6:00 game. I'm screaming down Euclid in my '72 Super Beetle, most likely listening to Boston, Foreigner or Chicago on 8-track. I pass my high school and guess who's waiting for me? Martinez. This time, 45 in a 25, at 5:17 p.m. At least I improved my speed control slightly.

I'm Dying

Have you ever had something happen with your body that's never happened before and it makes you believe you're dying? A few years back I flew into Cleveland on business. It was winter and very cold. I rented a car and started driving towards my hotel, about 30 minutes east of the airport. About 10 minutes into my drive I start to feel a warm sensation in my innards and lower back. At first I think it might be a kidney stone. I'd had a kidney stone about 10 years prior and it was horrific. If it was a kidney stone, I needed water. I learned from experience and the suggestion of my doctor to drink a boatload of water when you first feel like a kidney stone has made its presence known.

I don't have any water with me so I start looking for an off ramp with a gas station or a small store. The sensation of warmth has now increased to high heat. It felt like my anus was on fire. I am literally sweating and squirming around in my seat and as the heat and pain increase, it doesn't feel like a kidney stone, but I don't know what it is. I don't know what death feels like, but I was pretty sure I was heading there. *We are here today to celebrate the life of Dave McNichols, who died a horrible death from anus fire.*

I'm almost in a state of panic at this point, squirming, trying to stay focused on driving, and wondering what is happening to my body. Out of the corner of my eye I suddenly notice something in the car that I had not seen before: a button with the diagram of a seat, with a red light on. Light bulb goes on in my brain. A seat warmer, on high, burning a hole in my ass!

I was born and raised in the west. We don't have or need seat warmers. I'd never owned a car with one and had never used one before. I quickly turned it off and thanked God that I wasn't dying.

STUPIDITY BREAK

Grinder Haven

One of my all-time favorite eateries is one that my stupid brother turned me on to: The Grinder Haven in Ontario, CA. They make their own bread and make a fantastic pastrami sandwich.

Apparently they've become very benevolent with customers who order a combo.

HAVEN BURGER COMBOS

All Hamburger Combos come Ships or Fries And Medium Drink

Yogurt

My typical breakfast routine when I'm not traveling is either a piece of toast with peanut butter and chocolate milk, or a Yoplait yogurt, usually blackberry, along with orange juice. When I'm traveling and departing first thing in the morning I usually go for the yogurt choice since it's fast and easy. One Monday morning I was set to travel to Philadelphia, so after showering and getting dressed I head for the fridge to grab a quick yogurt. We were all out of Yoplait but we had several of another brand, which is Cindy's choice. I grab one, knock it down chased by some orange juice, then head out the door for the airport.

My flight schedule was from Ontario to Phoenix, switch planes, then on to Philadelphia. We take off from Ontario and I start to feel some discomfort in my body, like I am developing a hemorrhoid. Hemys aren't common for me so I am a little confused as to what might have caused it since I have not been having any issues in that area. The irritation increases as we get closer to Phoenix. It was like a group of anal Martians were tickling my anus and I couldn't do anything about it. It wasn't like

I could just do a reach-around to scratch it or anything, so I knew that I needed to do something when I got to Phoenix.

After landing I make my way to the little convenience store in the terminal to see if they have Vaseline, which they did not. I go into the men's room and wet a towel, then go into a stall to complete the reach-around and see if I can calm down the area. It helps.

I get on the flight headed to Philadelphia, which is about four hours. The irritation gets worse as time goes by. Horribly uncomfortable. When I arrive in Philly I get my rental car and head west for the 90-minute drive to my destination. My first stop before the hotel is Rite-Aid for some much needed Vaseline. Soon after, I check in to my hotel and get to my room to lube up the affected area...ahhhhh. After nine hours of anus fire I finally have some relief. I call my wife to check in and I tell her what happened. Her first question: "What did you have for breakfast?" "We're out of my yogurt so I had yours," I said. She then explained that her yogurt was Activia, a special high fiber blend. Dear God, that had to be it. I don't need fiber. I once had a Kashi bar and thought I might have to call 911.

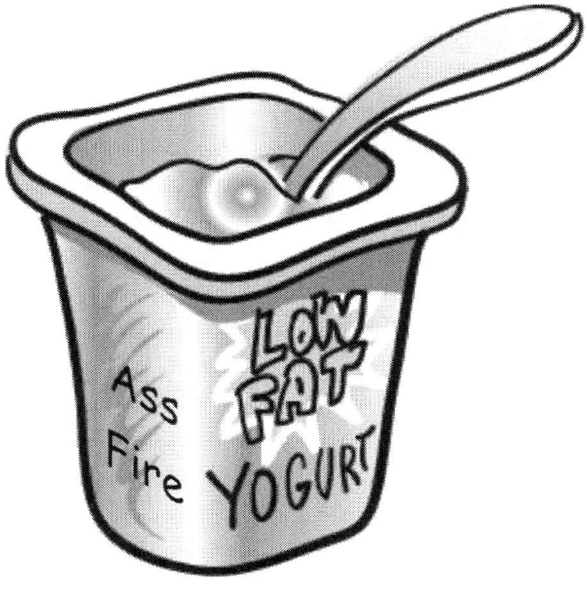
LOW FAT
Ass
Fire
YOGURT

Rental Cars

Once on a business trip to Denver I arrived at the Hertz Gold board, found my name and headed to my car, a Nissan Altima Hybrid. It was the first hybrid I had driven. After loading my luggage in the trunk I notice that I don't have a key, just a keyless key fob. I look on the dash to see a push-button starter, another first for me. I push the button, but nothing happens. Not a sound. I push it again, nothing. I push it a third time, nothing. So I open the glove box to obtain the manual. At the same time someone knocks on my window. It's a Hertz representative. "Sir, do you have any questions?" he says.

"Yes I do," I say. "I've pushed the start button three times but the car isn't starting."

He responds very nicely, obviously knowing what a dumbass I am. "Sir, the car is on. It's a hybrid so you'll only hear the engine when it needs to build power. It's running on electricity right now."

"Oh," I say, "Thank you"...closes window, hides red face, and sheepishly drives out of parking lot.

A few months later I arrived in Sacramento, checked the Hertz Gold board, and arrived at my assigned car...another hybrid. I think, *Ah ha! I've got this one.* Later that day I take a couple associates to lunch. While we are in the restaurant a couple other associates of ours arrive to meet us. As they approach our table one of them asks if any of us has a red Nissan Altima rental car. I do and acknowledge as such. He then tells me that they parked next to it and found the engine running. Apparently when I pulled up and parked, the engine wasn't making any noise so I failed to turn it off. I quickly went to the parking lot and turned it off. These days I know how to work a hybrid.

Driver's License

Back in my high school days we had a class for driver's education, with book training and actual simulators. I passed the class, then got my learner's permit at $15\frac{1}{2}$. For further training my dad took me to the church parking lot in his '72 Ford LTD. There weren't any cars in the lot that day so we had the run of the place. My dad starts off by showing me how do a Brody, where you floor it from a stopped position while turning sharply. That was fun. I take over and maneuver that beast of a car slowly around the parking lot while avoiding the many lampposts.

I eventually got my driver's license on my 16th birthday. Had to take the written test twice, but passed the driving test...barely. After obtaining my actual license I drove my mom home, then headed out for my first solo flight in the yellow LTD. I pull out of the driveway, make two right turns and am on San Antonio Avenue. I make it to 11th Street before running a stop sign. So that means I stopped at 8th, 9th, and Arrow Highway (same as 10th) before I failed. Not bad for a dumbass.

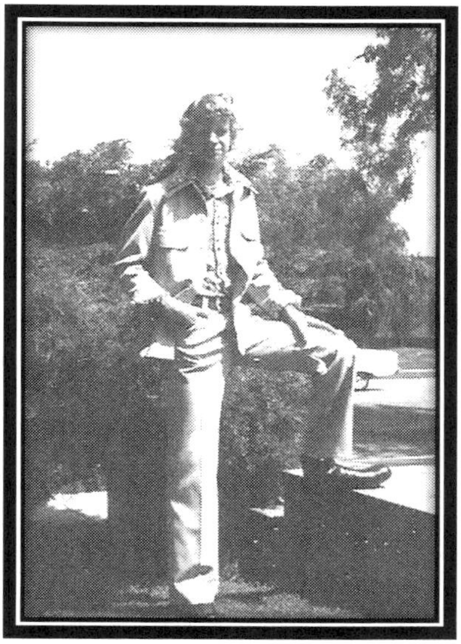

STUPIDITY BREAK

Zip It

My buddy Tim Schrader has had the pleasure of witnessing two of my "Stupidity" stories, "Golf" and "Jesus Paid..." from this book. When I called him to see if we could get a picture of ourselves at the golf course for this book he advised that he already had one, on a book shelf in his office, which is the picture prominently displayed on page 65. During this conversation, as we were talking about stupidity, he relayed a story to me, which is perfect for this book.

Tim's company designs warehouse systems and offers consultation in the supply chain industry. They designed a racking and motion system for a distribution company and were on site for day one of the install. One of the workers installing the racking took a quick break to use the restroom — for #1 — and apparently was in a big hurry to get back to work. He was in such a hurry that he zipped up his Levi's without putting his Johnson back where it belongs.

The zipper caught part of his member and zipped it up nice and tight. He ran from the bathroom in excruciating pain, screaming for help. Other workers rushed to help him, including his brother who was also on the crew. Everyone was unsure of how to help.

They couldn't just unzip it. His brother had a great idea and ran for his toolbox to retrieve his box cutters. (When Tim first told me this, I cringed and had to hold myself thinking of what might have happened.) The brother cut a hole in the Levi's, an exact circle surrounding the zipped-up penis. This did nothing to solve the problem. 911 was called.

Tim remembers that once the paramedics and firemen arrived, they all stood in a circle staring at the injured subject, with a perfect circle of his pants cut out to expose the biggest fear of all men in history, from the invention of the zipper until now.

They had no idea what to do to rectify the situation, so they loaded him up in an ambulance and took him to the hospital.

Apparently the emergency room doctor knew what to do, because three hours later this worker returned to finish his day, wearing the same pants, minus the denim that used to cover the hole.

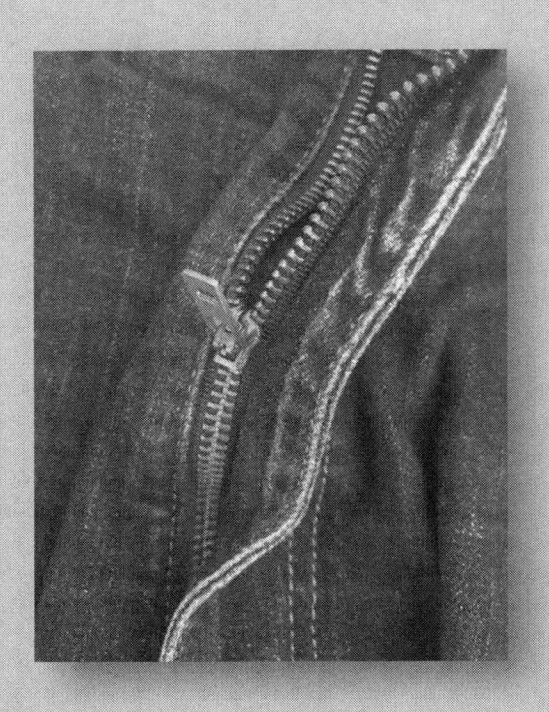

Chapter 2

My Life In Music And Stupidity

Beginning Drums

One good thing that my stupid brother did for me at a young age was turn me on to great music, which included The Beatles, Elton John, and Chicago. I would listen for hours and the drums stuck out for me. Ringo Starr, Nigel Olsson, and Danny Seraphine were the respective drummers. My favorite albums were *Abbey Road*, *Sgt. Pepper's Lonely Hearts Club Band*, Elton John's self-titled album, *Tumbleweed Connection*, *Honkey Chateau*, and Chicago's first album, *CTA*.

I started putting together a make-shift drum set from things I found in the house so I could bang out some rhythms. Varied sizes of pots and pans from the kitchen for toms, a frying pan upside down for a good snare drum, pan lids hanging from a shelving bracket with string around the knobs for cymbals, then the kitchen trash can upside down as a floor tom, which makes a great *thud*. I used wooden spoons as drum sticks. It sounded horrible, but it was all I had...until my mom started to prepare dinner and couldn't locate half the stuff she needed. My parents sensed that I wasn't going to give up my quest to play drums so they took me to a music store to investigate the idea of getting a drum set. They consulted with the proprietor who helped them make a very wise decision. He knew that kids go through fads and give up on things quickly so he suggested a set of sticks and a practice pad. "If he keeps to it for a while and looks like he's not going to give it up, look into a set of drums at that point and some lessons." He could have talked them into a set and made a sale, but instead he did the right thing.

I kept at it and joined the concert band in junior high. This is where I learned basic rudiments, how to play in time, and how to read music. By the end of the 6th grade I was the first chair percussionist. With all this great momentum as a musician I did the smart thing for the 7th grade: I signed up for wood shop instead of band. Brilliant. On the first day of school I was sitting on a stool in wood shop, waiting for class to start when someone grabbed my shirt at my shoulder from behind. "McNichols, get in the band class. You're my first chair drummer. You're not taking wood shop." It was the band director. So ever since that day I've had trouble making things with wood, but I can play a paradiddle.

Eventually my parents bought me a real drum set and gave it to me as a Christmas gift. In the pic below I'm showing off my new kit to my cousins.

L-R: Jeff Goodwin, Beaker, Brad Goodwin, Dog, Tami Goodwin

Beaker

When I was in elementary school, I somehow gained the nickname "Pickle." Pickle McNichols. I'm sure a fellow third grader was very proud to give me that name. I hope he's currently serving time. I didn't like the nickname. Every time I was called it, or some variation, it seemed degrading. I carried that nickname all the way through high school, then it finally died off.

In 1980 I had been out of high school for a couple years and was playing a lot of music with a new friend, Dwayne Condon. Dwayne had become my closest friend and would eventually support me as the best man in my wedding.

We had taken over my parents' house for a week while they were on vacation, setting up the living room as our band room. Dwayne on keys (including a Fender Rhodes "Dyno"), Randy Goff on bass, and me on drums. We would jam for hours, then Randy would make us a fantastic dinner, and we'd watch TV to wind down.

One night, we were watching *The Muppet Movie*. What else would twenty year olds do in the eighties? Dwayne looked at the screen, looked at me, then pointed at the character Beaker and said, "Hey, he looks like you." My new nickname was born.

Beaker and Dwayne Condon

At the time, I was tall and skinny and had poofy hair, just like Beaker. I still have the nickname, I'm just not as tall as I used to be.

Some of my friends shorten it to Beak. Maybe they're in a hurry. My long time buddy Smitty Price turned it into Beakman, and on a few occasions has called me Beakman Turner Overdrive, because I take care of business. Look that one up if you don't get it.

When my wife, Cindy, and I started dating, she didn't know my real name for several weeks. She knows it now.

Elvis

When I was a senior in high school I heard that Benny Hester, a Christian musical artist that I liked, was going to do a concert at another local school. I went to the concert and he had a full band of great musicians and put on a great concert. When they were done and starting to pack up, I wanted to go up and meet the drummer. He was a big burly guy, about 40 years old, with a big beard. I went up to him and asked if I could help pack up and move his cases out to his car. He said sure; his name is Ron.

As I was helping him pack up I noticed that all his cases were stenciled with the name *Elvis Presley Show*. As we were pushing his rolling cases out to the parking lot I said, "I see that your cases have *Elvis Presley Show* on them. Do you play for one of those Elvis impersonator shows?"

He stops pushing his cases, looks up at me and says in a very annoyed tone, "I played for Elvis for 10 years." Oops. It was Ron Tutt, a very famous drummer. This was widely known except to an idiot like me.

Ron Tutt playing drums with Elvis Presley

Senior Recital

Back in good old 1985 I was hired for a gig playing drums for a senior recital of a student at Citrus College in Glendora, CA. Cindy and I were engaged and were inseparable, so I invited her to join me.

I can't remember the guy's name who hired me or what instrument he played, but I definitely remember the performance directly before ours. We showed up early for a rehearsal and took a seat in the front row so I could be close when it was my turn to play. This was senior recital time and there was a long list of performers. The groupings weren't typical. The students had the freedom to invite almost any other instrumentalists they wanted, and would perform either an original composition or a cover of another composer's work. There were string quartets, duos of guitars, singers, pianists, and various other combinations.

The musicianship was at varied levels and many of the performances were rough or boring. We sat there in the front row, waiting my turn, for what seemed like forever. Finally we were getting closer. The group before mine approaches the stage. Three instrumentalists: a trombonist, a flautist and a violinist. I am enthralled. They set up three chairs in a semicircle with music stands in front of each. They sit, count off, and start playing. What they were playing, I'm not sure. It seemed to be continuous nonsense of alternating quarter notes between the trombone and flute with the violinist playing some sort of drone underneath. It was painful to say the least. I figure I need to do something to lighten it up for Cindy and me so I pretend to pull something from my nose and start strumming it, like an imaginary guitar playing in time with the so-called music coming from the stage.

Cindy thinks it's humorous and she gets the giggles. Since we're in the front row she's trying to stop to be respectful of not only the performers, but also the friends and family sitting behind us. Watching her with the giggles gets me going and now I've got the giggles and I'm trying to do everything in my power to hold it in. It's like the scene from *The Mary Tyler Moore Show* when they're at the funeral for Chuckles the Clown and Mary gets the giggles. Cindy is still giggling and every time I look at her it gets worse for me. Every muscle that controls my bladder is in DEFCON 1, and a launch is impending. I'm holding it in so hard that I proceed to wet my pants and not just a little. I unload my bladder into my white cotton pants. *Dear God, what am I going to do now?*

The trio finally completes their underwhelming performance and now I have to go up on stage. There's no time or opportunity to do anything else, like go buy a new pair of pants, or take mine off and dry them in the sun while I sit somewhere in my underwear. I have to get up, walk in front of a hundred people, show them I have wet myself, then sit behind the drums and attempt to play and support someone's shining moment as he graduates from college. Someone I can't even remember. I stand up, red-faced, back to the crowd, and attempt to cover the huge wet spot with my stick bag as I make my way up to the stage. That was the easy part. What I was really worried about was exiting the stage when I was done. *Would it dry up by then? How could I cover it inconspicuously?*

Somehow I got out of there without too much embarrassment and once Cindy and I were outside we laughed our asses off! It still makes us laugh today. I am such a dumbass.

Pictures With Presidents

Sometime around 1985 I was in a band with a great buddy of mine, Mike Lizarraga. Mike is a fantastic guitarist and bassist. Mike's parents lived in a huge, beautiful home on a hill overlooking the San Dimas-Glendora area. Mike's dad, David, was the president of a development company and was also involved in many charitable foundations. David's work also connected him to the political arena, which led to him being involved with many politicians at a very high level.

We were rehearsing one day at Mike's parents' house and that was the first time I had been there. On a break I walked down a hallway to use the restroom and noticed several pictures on the wall, so I was checking them out. The first picture was David with President Nixon. The next picture was David with President Carter. Hanging next to that was a picture of David with President Ford. Then another one of David with President Reagan. At the time, I didn't know anything about what David did for a living and I thought it would be out of the realm of possibility that he had met and taken pictures with four presidents. Just then, Mike walks down the hall and I say, "Hey, did your dad go to one of those places where you can take pictures with a cardboard standup of famous people?"

Mike's response: "No, you dunce, he's met and done work for the last four sitting presidents." My bad. Further evidence of my brilliance.

How Does This One Go?

Along with being a management professional these days I'm also a professional musician and have been for many years. Back in my younger days I happened upon a southern gospel quartet called The Californians at a gig and they asked me to start playing with them. I agreed and some stupid stuff happened.

This is where I learned to think on my feet, or drum chair, while on a gig. The Californians had no set list. We would take the stage, someone would call out a tune and we'd start playing. The first time this happened I was freaking out.

I didn't know any of these songs and never listened to this style of music. I would look to the guitar player or bass player and say, "How does this go?" and they would just start playing. Once I heard the groove I had it. And it turned out that every song basically sounded the same and had the same format. There was no chance that an odd time signature would break out.

L-R: Top – Beaker, Brian Masterson, Phil Jester
Bottom – Dale Peters, Chris Foster, Dave Coleman

Do You Guys Know Anything About Jazz?

Eventually the group decided to change the format from a quartet to a Christian band fronted by one singer. The new band name was Access. We went in the studio and recorded an album of original music, mostly done at Soundhouse in Hollywood and the now defunct Weddington Studios in North Hollywood, CA.

While laying a track down at Soundhouse, a guy walks into the engineer's booth and is talking with our producer, Smitty Price. Soon after, this guy with long stringy hair and a rock-and-roll weathered face walks into the studio where we are: Dave Coleman on guitar, Chris Foster on bass, Mark Stephens on keyboards, and me on drums. He walks up to us and asks if we know anything about jazz. We kind of chuckle at the randomness of the situation, and then Dave responds by saying that he has a degree in music and understands some jazz theory. The rest of us kind of nod in agreement, as we start to realize this might be a producer who wants to hire us for a record date. The guy tells us he's looking for rock musicians who are not influenced by jazz for his upcoming album and tour.

He says thanks and leaves. We all looked bewildered as we questioned who this was. It was Larry Norman, a pioneer in Christian rock.

L-R: Beaker, Brian Masterson, Dale Peters,
Phil Jester, Chris Foster, Dave Coleman

Naked Baby

After our brush with Christian rock fame, the album was completed and pressed. I don't remember hearing about or getting involved in the design for the album cover, or whose idea it was, but it might rank as one of the worst of all time.

Fuel

The Californians were somewhat ahead of their time back in the 1970's, traveling from gig to gig in a former Continental Trailways bus that had been converted with sleeping bunks in the back and a lounge in the front with a killer sound system. We loved just hanging out in the lounge with the stereo cranked. There was a bathroom on the bus, but we were told never to use it. Not sure why. Maybe there was a scientific experiment being conducted in there.

Our manager had a deal to purchase fuel at a reduced rate from a friend who owned a trucking company in Santa Fe Springs. At rehearsal a few nights before we headed out for a weekend of gigs, our soundman, Phil Mata, and I are elected to take the bus down and fuel it before the trip. On Friday morning Phil and I head out for the 30-minute drive. When we arrive we park in the middle lane, in between the pumps, then go inside for the key.

We place the diesel nozzle in the tank and start filling. Shortly thereafter I notice that there is another tank on the other side of the bus and a pump right next to it. I suggested to Mata that if we fill both sides simultaneously we'll be done in half the time. He thinks it's a great idea and we commence with our plan.

What we don't know is that one of the pumps is diesel; the other is regular. The 80's kind of regular, which could burn a hole in your shoes. We're so excited to be completing our assigned task quickly that we don't notice the difference.

Once we're done we head north and almost make it all the way back before the regular fuel eats through the lining of the fuel tank, clogging the filter. The bus stops on a dime in heavy traffic. Dale comes to the rescue and is able to diagnose, then clear the filter and get the bus back to his house. We had trouble with the fuel filters being clogged for years due to our genius idea, but I don't remember ever being asked to fuel again.

Sliced American Cheese

To support the release of our album Dale started booking live dates. We had hopes of playing for some good audiences, selling albums and making a little money. The trouble was that Dale's contacts were mostly those who liked and wanted to hear their southern gospel favorites, and this was pop rock. Dale is a great man of God and a great guy. I know he has a knack for four things: 1. Booking dates. 2. Not telling us the whole story prior to the gig. 3. Finding a Bob's Big Boy on every trip. 4. Breaking into churches and venues if the key holder was late or we were early. Here's a pic of Dale teaching me how to break in.

One of the shows he booked for Access was a Saturday night concert at a large church in the thriving Central California metropolis of Madera. Soon after our fueling experience we board the bus with our gear and head north from Glendora.

Dave Coleman and Beaker

We arrive in Madera around 2:00 p.m. to find a beautiful building with a setting in the round and a great sound system. We break in, set up, and sound check. The pastor arrives and tells us that they have been playing our album on local radio and really promoting the concert. He is looking forward to a big crowd. Things couldn't have sounded and felt better and we are excited for the evening's show.

About seven people show up. We play the show with all the energy we have, the pastor speaks, one person accepts Christ and becomes a Christian, we break down, load the bus and wait in the bus lounge while Dale is finalizing things with the pastor. We all agree that if at least one soul is saved or blessed by our message then the trip is worth it, and we are getting paid.

Dale and the pastor finish their conversation and Dale enters the bus with a couple boxes in his hand. He explains that due to the low attendance the pastor could not pay us. The pastor felt bad, so in lieu of cash gave us two boxes of government-issued American cheese from his food for the poor program. One six-pound brick for everyone, sliced.

As we drive out of the church parking lot, disgusted and pissed off, our guitar player Dave goes into the bus bathroom (the same one we were told never to use) and pulls the lever opening the chute and dispensing 15 years of human waste. Half of it onto the church parking lot, the other half on the under carriage of the bus. We all yell like pirates who have just ravaged the seas and shortly after we fully understand why we were told never to use the bathroom and NEVER to pull the lever. That was the worst odor known to man and now our bus was wearing it proudly for the next 200 miles for us to enjoy. We still enjoyed our dinner at Bob's Big Boy.

L-R: Mark Stephens, Lee Bomgardner, Beaker, Brian Masterson, Chris Foster, Henry Boehm, Dave Coleman

Monopoly And Dr. Pepper

Speaking of human waste, we once finished a summer show in Phoenix and were making the seven-hour drive along I-10 in the hot afternoon sun. As we sat in the lounge, chilling out, Chris and I broke into a game of *Monopoly* while seated at the table with bench seats facing each other. I was facing the front with Chris across from me, his back to the driver.

Dale has to relieve himself (#1) but obviously can't use the bathroom on the bus and doesn't want to delay our trip by stopping, so he fills a Dr. Pepper can. He announces this as he approaches us from the back of the bus, offering a warm drink to anyone interested, holding the can in the air as a prize. We tell him to get away from us and get rid of that can. Dale decides that the best way to dispose of the can is to throw it out a window into the desert. As he opens the window behind Chris, the wind immediately blows our *Monopoly* money all over the bus, so we start yelling at him to close it. He attempts to throw the can of his warm urine out the window, but the can strikes the frame, turns towards us, empties the liquid into the air and the wind blows it all over Chris' back and my face. Lovely. Game over, urine wins.

A Cleansing

For this band, it seemed as if Central California was a special place. We had an annual gig at a church in Visalia. The church was always packed and the people were friendly and welcoming. One time we arrived late for our performance and were rushed to set up and sound check. Since we were short on time, someone offered to grab food for us while we were sound checking and have it ready before the service. McDonald's was the choice. Burgers, fries, cokes.

Chris was just ending his annual purging and fasting body cleanse during this trip so McDonald's wasn't on his menu, but he was hungry like the rest of us. I never really understood the necessity of these purges, since it appeared that every impurity in his body would manifest itself on his face. He would look like he'd been run over by a truck, in the name of health.

After sound check we all pound multiple burgers and fries washed down by Coca Cola, then within minutes we are up onstage doing our set. I am feeling good. This was my regular diet at the time. At about the third song of the set I notice people in the front row acting weird, with worried expressions on their faces. I turn just in time to see Chris move his bass inward as he throws up fully facing the crowd. A total unplanned purge. He removes his bass and exits stage left while we finish the song in total horror of what just happened.

The song ends and I immediately go back stage to see how Chris is doing. He's laughing about what just happened. He feels great now. He cleans up while others have cleaned up the stage. We go back on stage and start the next tune and you'll never guess what happens again. I guess the first purge didn't clear everything. One more time for good measure. Chris did not return to the stage again that night. A year later we returned to play our annual concert to find the stain on the carpet still there.

Chris Foster

Gone Fishing

Other than playing music, sometimes we got together just for fun. One time Dale arranged a deep sea fishing trip. We all met at Dale's house and took the bus down to Newport Beach and boarded an all-day fishing boat. We all caught a few and later that night took the bus back to Dale's. We didn't have any gigs the next weekend so two weeks later I come rolling up to Dale's early on Saturday and I see all of the guys standing outside of the bus. I was the last one there. I park and walk up to them to find that they're all complaining about a horrible stench coming from inside the bus. Apparently someone left their fish in the bus two weeks prior, and after they compare notes, that someone happened to be me. I was then awarded the task of removing said fish from the bus. It was not pleasant.

Horsey Video

Attempting to promote our new album, Dale somehow got us booked on a Christian television program at The Trinity Broadcasting Network. This network had a series of shows with special guest speakers and guest musical artists. We were excited. Then we were told that this was one of their low budget shows with minimal sound and lighting production, so we couldn't play as a live band. Instead, the band members would have to stand around a piano, with Dale faking like he was playing and the rest of us with mics in our hands lip-syncing. This sounded crazy. Neither I, nor Chris or Dave was used to standing and singing with a mic. We were used to being behind our instruments.

Well, the show must go on, so we came up with a plan to rehearse as a quartet around a piano, to get used to the feeling. We all went shopping and got suits to ensure we presented ourselves properly. This was the early 80s, so camera gear and video machines weren't easy to come by. Dale was friends with the owner of the local video rental store and was able to borrow some equipment from him so we could videotape our rehearsal and watch ourselves to critique and improve. The video storeowner loaned Dale a camera and a Beta Max player and he gave Dale a box of used tapes and said Dale could tape over any of them.

We had rehearsal at Dale's house around the piano in his living room. With some makeshift lighting and the recording gear, it was like a mini TV production studio. We did a few run throughs with our singer Carl, Chris, Dave and me standing around Dale at the piano. Obviously, Carl was very comfortable standing with a mic and singing. It's what he did. Not so much for the rest of us, so Dale and his wife Gail would watch and help direct us to move a little more and try to look natural. We recorded a couple run throughs of the song, then Dale moved the gear to the family room to hook up the Beta Max to his TV.

He got the player hooked up and we all gathered around the TV to watch. Dale, Gail, their 11-year-old daughter Michele, their 9-year-old son Michael, Chris, Carl, Dave, our sound tech Phil, and me. We were all excited because in the early 80s it wasn't common to have this gear and actually videotape. Dale hits play and the first thing we see is a horse doing nasty things to a beautiful blond. We all watch in horror. I'd never dreamed of anything like this, let alone seen it. It burned a horrible impression onto my eyeballs and brain. Apparently the tapes that were given to Dale had some crazy stuff on them and Dale didn't rewind all the way when he started recording.

After the horse was done we rewound the tape and started over. After several takes and instruction we all became experienced singing performers. Our performance on TV was underwhelming and we never became famous. The moral of the story: Don't feel too bad for horses.

STUPIDITY BREAK

Tacet

"Tacet" is Latin for "it is silent." It is a standard term used in musical notation to indicate not to play.

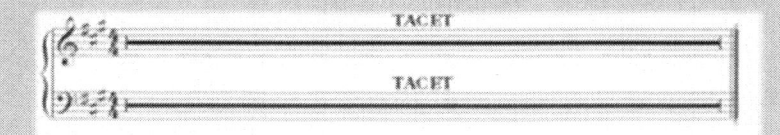

Back in the good ole early 90s I was hired for a gig by a close friend of mine, Dwayne Condon, who was conducting a musical with a large choir and a small orchestra, including me on drums and one of my best friends, Felix, on bass. Felix is a great bass player, although at the time he was not the most proficient at reading music. The pieces of music chosen for this show were all notated and not up for improvisational interpretation. As a musician on this gig your job was to play what was written.

We show up for our first rehearsal and are given the sheet music for each piece. The first piece is approximately 32 pages long.

The notation for the rhythm section is *Tacet* for the first 18 pages. This means we need to read the chart along with the rest of the orchestra, while they play and we don't.

So we're ready to start, 50 in the choir and 20 of us in the orchestra...and Felix. Dwayne counts us off... "1-2-3-4..." and Felix starts playing. Dwayne stops everyone. "Let's try that again," he says. "1-2-3-4..." and Felix starts playing again. Dwayne stops again. "Felix, you have *tacet*," he says.

Felix looks at his music, moves the first piece out of the way and looks behind it, like he's going to find either the holy grail or a piece of music that matches what he just played, which was wrong.

I say to him, "Tacet."

"What's tacet?" he says.

"It means don't play," I answer.

"Oh," says Felix. We laugh, quietly, as Dwayne counts it off again. I tell Felix not to play until I give him the sign.

When we spoke about it after rehearsal and I asked him why he just started playing, he said he didn't see any notation for bass until the 19th page, so he just started there.

Jesus Paid It All

For many years I've been playing gigs on weekends and for about the last 10 years I've been playing a couple weekends a month at a local church, Hillside Community Church. My longtime friend Smitty Price is the music director there. They have one Saturday night service and two Sunday morning services. The music at Hillside is contemporary to modern style worship, so for those who aren't familiar with this it's a full rock-style band fronted by a singer. Typically they'll have bass guitar, drums, keyboards, an electric guitar or two, an acoustic guitar, a lead singer and a few backup singers.

Smitty had planned a vacation one weekend and asked if I could MD (music direct) for him, which I agreed to. I would usually do this two to three times per year while he took time off. When Smitty is there he uses a click track to set tempos. Basically, it's a metronome controlled from his computer, which plays a constant *click* sound in our ear buds so everyone keeps in time. He'll start the click then count off the song. When he's away and I'm running things, I use a Boss Dr. Beat electric metronome, which is fed into everyone's ears and I have a mic to count things off.

This particular weekend we had a sub playing keys for Smit and his name is Nick. Nick is a pro and has played for a bunch of well-known artists like Stevie Wonder and Al Jarreau. One of the tunes we were doing is titled "Jesus Paid It All," as an offertory during offering. This song is in 3/4 time and we play it at 76 BPM (beats per minute). For the flow of this particular weekend's services we play two songs to start the service, and then the pastor comes up to give announcements and take an offering. The plan is for Nick to start playing "Jesus Paid..." quietly as the pastor prays before offering. I am supposed to lead him by giving him the count off. Well, the pastor starts to pray, then Nick just starts playing without my count, so I quickly start the click so he can line up with the tempo. It works.

Now, I have to clarify something here. When I programmed the click for all the songs of that weekend I did it in a rush. I thought I would have more time on Saturday, like I usually do, but being the music director caused me to be pulled into many different directions before rehearsal and sound check, so I was short on time.

When I programmed "Jesus Paid..." I set it on 3/4 time, but I doubled the BPM to 152 (76 x 2) so everyone would hear clicks in between the beats, to help keep them in time. This method is used when you have a slower tempo. My plan was to change it back to 76 after rehearsal and before sound check, but I didn't have time.

We played it perfectly in rehearsal and sound check. We did the mock prayer and counted Nick in; it all worked. Now we're in the service. Pastor starts praying, Nick starts playing, I start the click to line him up, and all is good. Now as soon as I hear the pastor say "Amen" I'm supposed to count the band in and we're off and running. "Amen." Now this is exactly the moment when I have a complete brain fart. I count us in at 152, not 76. Twice as fast. The band is dead on it. They come in at 152 just like I lead them to, like leading sheep to slaughter. *Oh no.* You knew right way that something was wrong. Nick starts to swing it a little because it feels like you have to at that tempo. I'm trying to get us back to the real tempo and feel, but not succeeding. Our woodwinds player, Steve Alaniz, is looking up at me from his sax wondering what the hell I just started. My buddy Tim Schrader, from my infamous "Golf" story in this book, is on guitar, and he just stops playing. Good idea. While we're playing the four-bar intro, one of the lead singers, Greg, turns around and looks at me and says in the mic, "Well, I guess we're going to swing it." So the singers start, and they swing. Everyone is swinging. A wonderful time for all.

    We tried for four minutes to get that tune back on the tracks, but couldn't do it. Train wreck. One of the lead singers is named Harmony. I wish I could have a picture of the look on her face – both bewilderment and fear. After we ended it and walked off stage for the message I walked back to the cafe and encountered the worship arts director, Gina. Her quote: "That was interesting. I don't think I've heard that version before." That version is now famous, thanks to me.

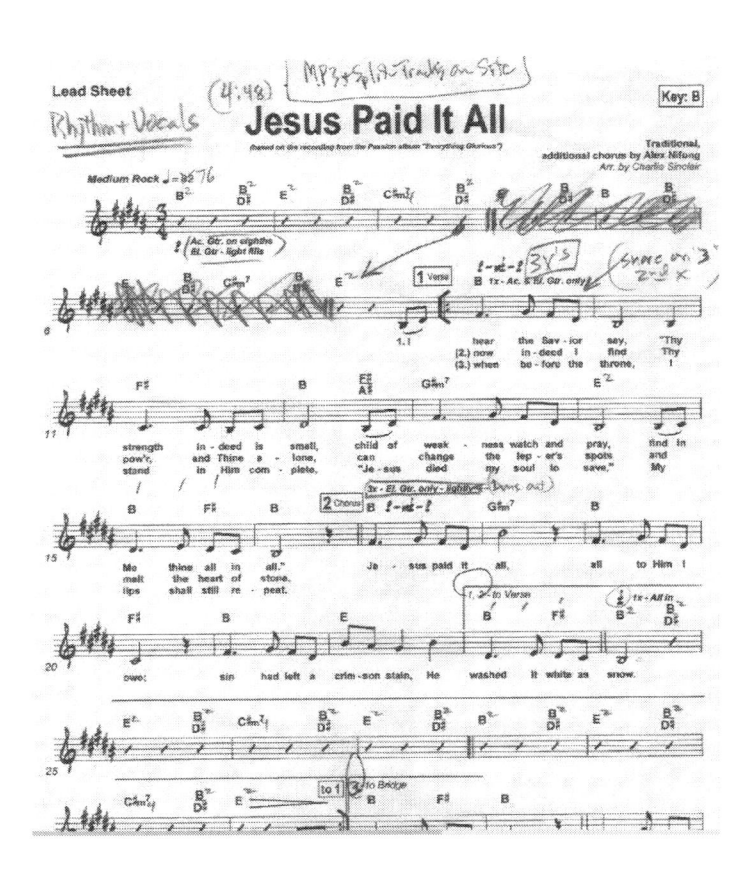

I Can't Hear

One of the tools of the trade I possess as a professional musician is a pair of sound isolating earphones. Shure SE215's. They're designed to fit into the ear canal and block most of the ambient noise, optimizing the sound. Each earphone has its own micro driver, which enhances the bass response. I use these for gigs and for listening to music while flying around the country.

One weekend I was playing at Hillside with my aforementioned friend Smitty. Both rehearsal and dress were great this particular weekend and we were ready to go. Two minutes prior to countdown I step onto the drum riser, plug my earphones into the monitoring system, and I'm ready to go. Countdown ends and Smitty counts in the first tune. I do a drum fill and we're off. Immediately I realize that I'm not hearing anything in my left ear, only the right. I'm unable to do anything about it because I'm obviously using both hands to play. During the first opportunity I have for a break in the song I wiggle the left cable, thinking the cable might be the issue, but nothing changes. Then we're into the next song and again, I'm busy with both hands.

After the second song there's a short break while the pastor does announcements, so I take advantage of the opportunity. I pull the phones off my ears, unplug the cable from the left ear piece, then plug it back in and test it. Nothing. No sound. Nothing else I can do at this point. This makes it very difficult to play. Back in the old days we had stage monitors blasting a mix of the band and vocals and no one wore headphones or earphones. These days, stage monitors have gone away for the most part, so the sound on stage is minimal. You hear the drums and maybe some guitar coming out of an amp that's covered up off stage. So at this point I've got sounds in my right ear but in my left ear I'm hearing live drums, which are drowning out the right ear. Very tough to hear the click track that I need to follow to keep everyone in line. We play a couple more songs after announcements, then we're on a break during the message. We head back to the green room.

  I sit down, remove my earphones and attempt to figure out what's wrong. I unplug the cable from both ears and switch them, then plug it into my iPhone so I can play some music and test it. Still no sound on the left side. Crazy. Smitty sees what I'm doing and inquires. He thinks maybe a driver blew out in the left earphone. Makes sense. He also tells me that Shure will repair it if it's still under warranty. I check the Shure website and find that the SE215's have a two year warranty. You can mail them the earphones with a copy of the receipt and they'll repair them and return them back to you. The next challenge was to find the receipt and see if I'm still under two years, which I figured I was.

    I borrow some earphones from the church to finish the weekend. When I get home Saturday night I search my receipt file but can't locate one. I bought them at Guitar Center so the next task is to search my Quicken check register to determine when I purchased them. I find the entry and it was 22 months back, still under warranty. On Monday I go to Guitar Center to see if they can reprint my receipt and fortunately they are able to do so. I go back home, download the repair request form, fill it out and list the problem as "possible blown driver." I mail the phones with a copy of the receipt off for repair. I pay for insurance, tracking, and expedited service. I select an option to return the repaired phones via Fed Ex, for a small fee, to expedite the process.

A couple days later I receive email confirmation that Shure has received the earphones and will start the repair process ASAP. Two days later I receive them at my doorstep. I was excited. I figured they replaced the driver and I was back in action. I open the box, place the phones in both ears, plug them into my phone and play some music. Nothing in the left ear, full volume in the right. *What is wrong with these people?* I am thinking. *I go through all that work to get a receipt, special shipping, extra shipping costs, and they send back the phones the same way I sent them: broken.* I was pissed. I go back to the box to see if there is a packing slip with information on it, and there is.

Under repair notes it states, "The loss of sound is due to earwax build up." *Oh. Hmmm.* I look at the left earphone and the small tube through which the sound travels along with the sleeve that covers it are full of earwax. I clean it out, and clean the right side too, and *wah lah*, the sound is perfect. Proving that I am a complete dumbass with dirty ears.

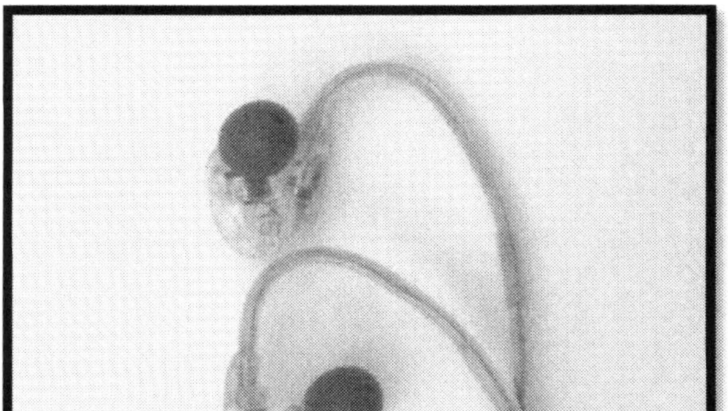

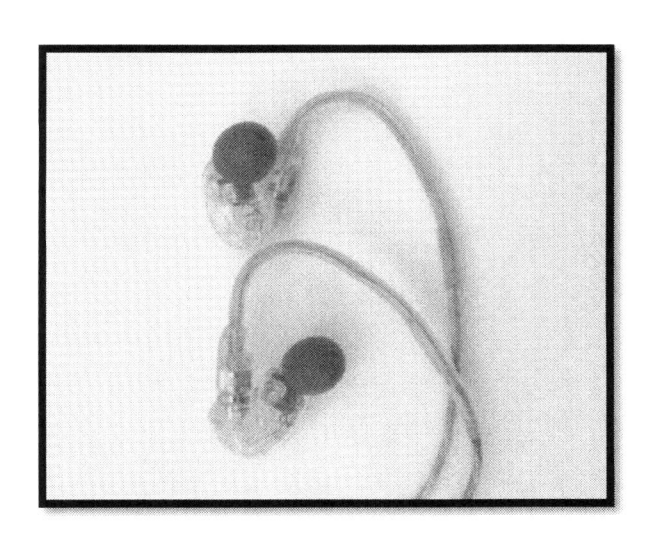

My First Recording Session

Qawwaaaaaaaaaaaaaww. I was on a flight between New York City and Southern California when I started this chapter. I leaned over to get something out of my bag and inadvertently typed the first thing you read. I decided to leave it.

It was somewhere around 1981. While doing a gig with The Californians I was approached by the owner of a studio who asked if I could do some recording work for him. He was working on an album for another gospel group and needed drums on it. I agreed. My first professional paid recording date. I was excited.

I was driving a very small Honda Civic at the time, which couldn't fit all my drums, so I kept my set on The Californians' band bus. I asked my band mate bass player friend Chris if I could borrow his truck. He agreed and we switched cars for a couple days.

Chris had a mid-sized truck with a shell over the bed. It was several years old and he was stringing it along. I met up with him the morning of the session to switch cars. He had several instructions for me about the vehicle. I had none for him, other than turn the key on and drive it. First of all, Chris' truck had a tendency to overheat. To combat this you had to turn on the heater. In addition, the driver's side window crank was broken so you couldn't roll down the window. It was mid-August. In mid-August it's really, really hot in Southern California. He said the fuel gauge didn't work, but it had plenty of gas. With that, we exchanged keys and I took off.

I had moved my drums back home with a couple trips in my little Civic because I needed to put new heads on them for the session. I load up my drums in Chris' truck then head out to the studio, which was about a 45-minute drive away. I stop by one of my favorite fast food restaurants to grab lunch, Mi Taco. Not for Mexican food, but for burgers. They had great burgers and fries. I get two cheeseburgers, large fries, and a large Dr. Pepper, and eat it in the car while driving. It was about 85 degrees outside that day at noon and heating up. I get about two miles down the freeway, slamming my food down, and I notice the temperature gauge rising. The car is heating up. I turn the heater on. Great. This should be fun.

I keep going towards the studio in Downey, finishing up my food and sweating profusely. The engine temperature is staying steady since I have the heater on full blast. As I approach the interchange at the 60 and 57 freeways the engine starts to miss, and chug, then it runs out of gas. I quickly pull over to the shoulder and stop. I'm pissed. It's almost 90 outside and it must be over 100 in the car because I have to run the stupid heater. Chris told me it had plenty of gas and within 20 miles I'm out. I step out of the truck and slam the door shut, and the window comes off its track and slides down into the doorframe.

These are the days long before cell phones, so I walk to a

call box. For those of you too young to know what one of these is, it's a box mounted to a pole on the side of the freeway, usually every 100 yards or so. In the box is a phone that, when picked up, automatically calls an operator who can help you get a tow truck or make a call to someone for help. I had AAA so I have the operator contact them. They dispatch a truck that arrives in about 20 minutes. I am starting to get nervous, not wanting to be late to my first session. The tow truck arrives with some gas to get me going again. That's when I discover that Chris has a locking gas cap to which I don't have the key. The tow truck driver has to break the cap off. He puts the gas in and I am back on my way.

At least the window is down now. I get back on the freeway, heater on full blast. 20 minutes later I arrive at the studio. I get my drums set up and the engineer gets them mic'd up. I play a little and tune them up for the room, and then we're all set. Now I can relax a little because I got there on time and I get to do some recording. The engineer tells me that the group I'll be recording for has already recorded their vocals and were accompanied by a pianist. The style of music is southern gospel.

He plays a little of the first song so I can get a feel for it. Pretty simple stuff, just a light beat required. There are no charts and no one there from the group to produce or give me guidance. They're leaving it up to me to play what I believe is the right thing for the songs. I go into the drum booth and put headphones on. He starts the first song and hits record. I come in at the appropriate place and start to play along with the pianist. Things are going well. About a minute in I feel a rumble in my stomach. Then the rumble moves south, and fast. *Uh oh.* I drop my sticks and run for the bathroom. It was a photo finish but I won, barely. Hello Mi Taco, I guess you've decided to leave.

Not feeling any more rumble, I finish up, wash up, and head back to the booth. I apologize to the engineer and we start over. He rolls tape, I come in and things are all good. I get one song done. Not too bad. Other than one sidebar, it went pretty smooth. He plays a little of the second song to give me the feel. Again, pretty simple. He rewinds, rolls tape and hits record. I'm in. First verse, second verse, first chorus. All of a sudden the pianist's time is fluctuating from slow to fast to slow. I have trouble lining up with it. The engineer stops and rolls tape back a little. He punches me in (hits record at a place in between beats to start recording over what I previously played) and I try it again. Not working. I'm really having trouble figuring out where it slows down, then speeds up.

He rolls tape back again and punches me in again. It's approaching the spot where the time gets funky and I'm concentrating really hard to try and catch it and move with it. Rumble, rumble. *Uh oh. Not again.* I drop my sticks again and hightail it to the bathroom. Unload version two. I guess Mi Taco only came to visit. I finish up and clean up, then head back into the booth. The engineer is being really cool about things. Lots of patience. We try the take again and I do all I can to follow the piano and it just doesn't work due to the lack of solid timing with the piano.

I'm really frustrated at this point. Car overheated, ran out of gas, hot and sweaty. All of this stress probably led to Mi Taco wanting to exit. I take off my headphones and go into the engineer's room. I say to the engineer something to this effect: "It's almost impossible to play to this crap. Did they ever think of using a metronome? This lady's time is horrible." In all my huff I don't think I noticed that another person had come in and was sitting next to the engineer. Then the engineer says, "Dave, this is Jim. He owns the group you're recording for today and he's one of the singers." Nice. Face turns red; humble pie eaten. I retreat to the booth and somehow play through the rest of the songs. They thank me. I break down, load up and depart. My first professional recording session, for which I never got paid.

Tacos

While writing the story about my first recording session, I remembered another one related to tacos. Fast-forward 22 years from the session described above. This one was at my good friend Dennis Moody's studio in the Mt. Washington area of Los Angeles.

We were putting drums on some tunes for an album being produced by another close friend, Terry Butler. It was a weekday, a Friday I believe. We started at about 10 a.m., got through a couple tunes pretty quick. Dennis makes it real easy. He gets great drum sounds very quickly.

We took a break around noon and went across the street for tacos — real tacos — at El Atacor, which I think means "ass blow" in Spanish.

The salsa in their tacos clears my sinuses. This is the type of place that makes authentic Mexican food. They have a jukebox that plays real Mexican music, and there's usually a Mexican soap opera on the TV. The Mexican soap operas all seem to play out the same way. Dude leaves his house. His wife hooks up with another dude. First dude suspects something and returns home to find his wife in bed with dude 2. Dude 1 points his gun at dude 2, then spends the next 25 minutes (with a break for two commercials) telling him off. Then he shoots him right at the end of the show, dramatic dying scene...commercial.

We all down a few tacos, chased with soda, then back to work. We finish up at about 2 p.m., then I break down and load up my car. I take off shortly thereafter trying to get in front of the rush-hour traffic, especially on a Friday. About 10 minutes into my drive I realize I have to go number 2. I didn't think it was bad enough to turn around and head back to the studio, so I just figured I could hold it until I got home. One thing I couldn't do was just stop any place and use their restroom because I had a car full of drums, and I had the hard drive which contained the whole album we were working on. I couldn't risk stopping at a public place, especially in the area I was in, and getting ripped off.

    I keep driving up the 110 freeway into south Pasadena and everything is fine. Then I have a contraction. *Uh oh.* What is it with taco places? I use the Lamaze breathing method to clear the contractions and hold off the birth, but I know I have to come up with a plan because waiting another 40 minutes to get home to the peace and comfort of my own bathroom is not going to happen. I get to the point where the 110 freeway ends in south Pasadena and take the Orange Grove Boulevard exit. This is how I get to the 210 freeway to get me home. I've had a couple more contractions at this point and can't hold it off much longer.

It's peeked at me a couple times and tapped on my shoulder. There aren't any services at this off ramp, just homes. And there aren't any services on Orange Grove between the two freeways, just homes.

I start heading north on Orange Grove trying to think of the closest place I can stop and not feel insecure with my car and the contents. I then remember that Lake Avenue Church is just one exit down after I get on the 210. I play drums at this church periodically and know exactly where the bathrooms are. In fact, this is the perfect place to stop because they have an underground parking area, which will be perfect to secure my car. As I'm going through more contractions, closer together, doing my Lamaze breathing, and in a cold sweat, I'm praying for green lights at Colorado, then the freeway entrance, then at Lake Avenue. Also, what if the church is closed on Fridays and locked up? You know how your body and mind work. If you decide you're going to use the bathroom somewhere, your mind can only control your body until the split second before you reach the toilet. No going back now, I'm heading to Lake Avenue.

The church is located on the north side of the freeway,

closest to the westbound lanes. I'm on the opposite side heading east. I exit the freeway and get a green light to turn left, and then another green light to turn left on the frontage road between the freeway and the church, then a right into the parking lot. We're at DEFCON 1 at this point. The launch sequences have been entered. I see a few cars in the parking lot — a good sign. I tear through the parking lot and take the ramp to the underground parking. I park right next to the elevator. I jump out, run to the elevator, squeeze my cheeks, press the elevator button; the door opens. Up one floor and 10 feet to my left is the men's room. It's unlocked. Another photo finish, but I won again. Life could not have been any sweeter after that was over.

Potato Salad

In the year 2000 we celebrated my 40th birthday by having a bash and a jam session with many of my friends. A couple of my friends, Felix Nunez and Kurt Dory, came and we played as a trio: Felix on bass, Kurt on guitar, me on drums. We had so much fun that we decided to continue playing together weekly. We found a local coffee house that would allow us to play each Tuesday night and we decided to cover tunes written by famed keyboardist David Garfield. David is the musical director for George Benson and has played for and recorded with many great artists for over 30 years. He fronted a couple well-known bands in the 70s and 80s comprised of the best studio musicians in the world; bands named Karizma and Los Lobotomys. We loved their music, jazz fusion, and decided to stretch ourselves by learning and playing it. We started our Tuesday night jam and after a month or so started to develop a small following.

Playing as a trio started to get old, missing a keyboard or second guitar, so Kurt suggested that we invite David Garfield to join us one night. Crazy idea. Invite one of our heroes? None of us knew him. I took on the task of attempting to contact him and found his website and sent him a note. I explained that we were just three guys with day jobs who were also professional musicians who were covering his music. I invited him to play with us one night and inquired as to his fee. He responded right away and was flattered and interested. We agreed on a number and he came out a couple weeks later. We packed the coffee house and had a great evening playing his music with our arrangements. He loved it and loved our vibe.

After the gig David suggested that we record an album together of these arrangements and some originals. We were astonished. We had just played with one of our heroes and thought that was the pinnacle; now another chapter in the story would be to record an album together. We wrote some originals and worked out more arrangements of David's tunes and recorded a live album at a famous jazz club in North Hollywood called The Baked Potato. David arranged for a couple special guest musicians to join us: Lenny Castro on percussion and Larry Klimas on woodwinds.

Larry plays with Elton John, Neil Diamond, The Manhattan Transfer, Chicago, and others. Lenny has played for just about everyone: Michael Jackson, Neil Young, Toto, Michael Buble, Pat Benatar, Barbra Streisand, and the list goes on, including the infamous hit by Toto, "Africa." By this time we had also added our friend Doug Nofsinger on guitar. It was a fantastic evening and the whole process was a great experience for us. Our project was titled *Potato Salad*, as a product of and homage to the club we recorded it in.

Our little *Potato Salad* project did very well in Japan and has sold all over the world. We've received communication that we're on radio playlists in various countries like Italy, Sweden, and parts of South America. Pretty good stuff for some knuckleheads from Rancho Cucamonga.

L-R: Doug Nofsinger, David Garfield, Felix Nunez, Lenny Castro, Beaker, Kurt Dohy

STUPIDITY BREAK

Special Mic & Wayne

Our Potato Salad live recording at The Baked Potato was made possible by the assistance of a Japanese company who was developing new technology for Sony. They were testing a new streaming technology and approached David Garfield, who offered the Potato Salad live recording night. We met with them and they offered to give us a hard drive with the live multitrack recording in exchange for allowing them to stream our show live to Japan. Deal.

The day of the show, while I was tuning and we were starting to run things down, I remember one of the Japanese guys micing my kit and he placed a mic pointing at my snare, but it was a good 12 inches away. I had never seen this before.

Normally the mic is placed just over the rim, just a few inches from the head. I asked him if we should move it closer, and he smiled and said "No, special mic." *Oh, it's a special mic...maybe some new technology.* It looked like an SM57 to me, but I left it.

After the show they gave David the hard drive with the raw tracks on it. They used recording software named Digital Performer, but we needed it in a different format and software — Pro Tools, so David reached out to an engineer friend Dennis Moody for assistance. Dennis wasn't able to do it but he referred David to an expert in this and his name is Wayne.

David spoke to Wayne and they agreed on a rate to transfer and format the files and arranged for a day when Wayne would complete the job at David's studio in North Hollywood.

On the fateful day, David met up with Wayne who explained that he was a big fan of David's music throughout the years and was looking forward to working on this project. David gave him some of his CDs and some shirts and they got Wayne all set up to start the process. He had the hard drive with the files in Digital Performer and a new hard drive with Pro Tools. Wayne explained that it was going to take about three to four hours. We had recorded two 90-minute sets that night at The Baked Potato, about 14 songs. Our plan was to select the best 9-10 tunes for the album. David told Wayne he would leave him to his work and would return later.

After about three hours, David returned, and no Wayne. No note from Wayne, and the CDs and shirts were still there. David called him, but it went to voice mail — several times.

At first David thought he might have gone to get something to eat. He checked the files to see if they had been transferred to the new hard drive. The first set, six tunes, had been transferred but the second set had not. He checked the original hard drive and nothing was on it — nothing. He checked the deleted file and nothing was in it — nothing. The second set was missing.

He called Wayne again. Voice mail. He then called Dennis and explained the status. Dennis called Wayne and reached him. Wayne admitted that he had screwed up and deleted the second set before transferring it, then deleted the deleted. Nice work, Wayne.

David took the hard drive to a company in Hollywood that specializes in retrieving deleted files. No go, nothing they could do... they were gone.

Dennis felt horrible, although he had nothing to do with Wayne's mistake, so he offered to have the band come to his studio and re-record some tunes to complete the album. What a guy, extremely generous in helping resolve the situation. We took him up on his offer and recorded three tunes live in the studio, then brought Lenny Castro back in to overdub some percussion. We then hired Dennis to mix the project.

Dennis Moody

When Dennis starting preparing the mixes he found that the "Special Mic" for the snare wasn't so special. The snare was barely audible so Dennis had to copy a snare sound from the studio session, then copy and paste it to every snare strike in the six tunes from the live recording. Tireless work. Dennis really came through for us. Wayne was never to be heard from again, and that special mic wasn't really that special.

L-R: Felix Nunez, David Garfield, Beaker, Doug Nofsinger, Kurt Dohy, Dennis Moody

Small Sausage

After mixing the *Potato Salad* project, the final step before having CDs created was mastering, where an engineer makes the final adjustments to the audio settings. Three of us attended the final mastering session: David Garfield, Felix Nunez, and me. Once the session was over we were handed a gold-mastered disc and our album was complete. As a celebration we decided to enjoy a nice dinner at a well-known Italian restaurant near the studio. Larry Klimas happened to live nearby so he was invited and joined us as well.

So there we sit in the restaurant, with Felix and I feeling like a couple kids in a candy store. We have just completed an album playing with some of our musical heroes and now are having dinner with them and they've become our friends. Felix and I aren't cool, but now we are hanging with the cool group and just trying to keep up. We order dinner. David, Larry, and Felix order pasta dishes, and I order a small sausage and cheese pizza. We have a great time conversing with David and Larry about the project, how it started, and how great it sounded. It was fun getting to know our new friends and getting to live on their level, for a short time anyway. We were on top of the world.

Then the waitress shows up with our food. "Who has the small sausage?" she says. I couldn't have put my hand up any quicker. She laughs and Felix starts laughing and just about wets his pants. David and Larry just stare at us like we're a couple dumbasses. Felix can't stop laughing and I'm just totally embarrassed. The "small sausage" jokes continue to this day, at my expense.

L-R: Beaker, Cindy McNichols, Larry Klimas, David Garfield

Chapter 3

My Brother Is Stupid

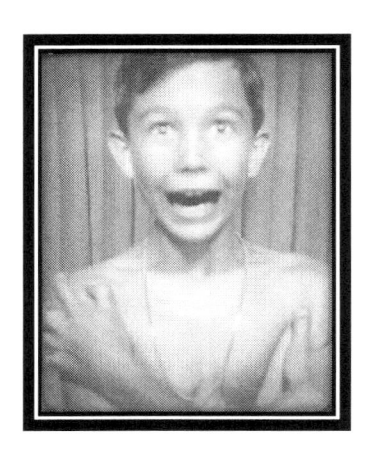

My Brother Is Stupid

My brother Mike is eight years my senior. He is much more higher educated than I. (Evident by the poorly worded sentence I just wrote). Is he more better than me? No. Here are some examples of what my stupid brother did to me when I was a kid. This is most likely why I have issues. And by the way, he considered getting a tattoo when he turned 50. Dumbass. Please let me know what the redeeming value of a tattoo is.

The Picture Window

What else would an eight-year-old have to do on a weekday afternoon, 1968, living in Southern California? Go in the front yard with a baseball and glove and play catch with himself. And what would this young boy's 16-year-old brother be doing at this same time? He would be standing on the roof of the house with his friend Kelly. Seems logical for my brother, since I'm sure the view from the roof of our suburban home in Southern California was similar to that overlooking the Caspian Sea.

L-R: Kelly Givens and my stupid brother Mike

Since there wasn't much to do on the roof for Mike and his friend, he requested that I throw my hard ball up to him on the roof. Knowing the strength and superb accuracy of my throwing arm, I quickly said no, but he persisted. Being of eight-year-old sound mind, I finally agreed. I wound up and aimed at my brother, who was standing directly above the 10-foot wide, 4-foot high picture window in front of our house. As my eyes stayed steady on the target, the ball went directly through the window.

Soon after this, my brother advised our mother that he had nothing to do with it.

Fire Extinguisher

When we were growing up, my brother and I shared a bedroom. We had matching twin beds, with the headboards against a wall and matching shelves above our heads. I was smart enough at 10 years old to know it wasn't a good idea to put heavy, unstable objects on my shelves, above my head, especially living in Southern California where earthquakes are routine. My brother, on the other hand, wasn't this smart.

On one of his trips to Newport Beach with his friends he found an old fire extinguisher, which must have fallen out of a boat. It had washed up on the beach and was full of sand. It had to weigh about 20 pounds. Where do you think my brother placed this new prized possession? On the bottom shelf above his bed, in late 1970.

On February 9th, 1971, at 6:01 a.m. PST we were awakened by the Sylmar earthquake. 6.5 on the Richter scale. It lasted 12 seconds. It caused mass destruction and 64 deaths, almost 65. The quake knocked the fire extinguisher off my brother's shelf and struck him in the head as he slept. I was hoping that it might knock some sense into him, but it's apparent that it didn't.

Oreo Cookies Grow In The Front Yard

What five-year-old boy wouldn't believe that Oreo Cookies grow in the front yard? This was the revelation my brother taught me one day. He encouraged me to try one. Not knowing that these supposed "Oreo Cookies" were actually tiny, blackish, hard and crusty morsels of dog shit, I excitedly picked one up and took a bite. Soon thereafter I learned that Oreo Cookies do not grow in the front yard, and I would guess not in the back yard either. When did I learn this? After the second bite.

Privacy

I have always enjoyed my privacy in the bathroom. No visitors. When I was about seven years old I was in the bathroom dropping the kids at the pool. I had not yet learned that I should lock the bathroom door. My stupid brother Mike and his friend Kelly were looking for something productive to do, so they grabbed a camera, opened the bathroom door and started taking pictures of me sitting on the commode. This is why I have issues.

"I'm Going Into The Navy"

When I was 11 years old my brother informed me that he had joined the Navy. He was 19. One day he tells me that we need to have a "brotherly" talk before he departs for boot camp. I thought this was a good idea. He tells me that this talk needs to happen in the back yard, so off we go. He then tells me that he needs to tie me up with some rope for this special talk. Again, I don't protest and allow it to happen. Once I am tied up, he turns on the hose and soaks me. He then proceeds to turn off the water and walk away.

"I'm Getting Out Of The Navy"

Nearing the end of my brother's tenure in the Navy he put together this little gem.

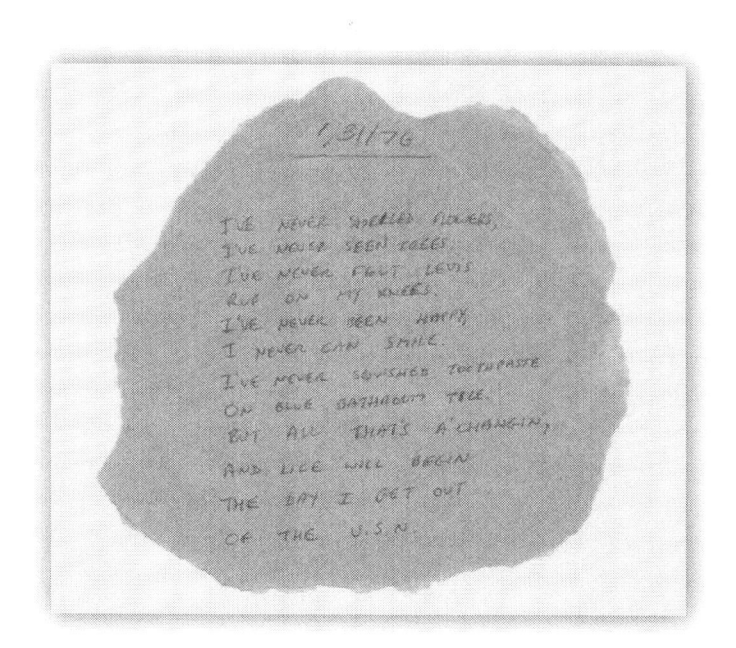

1/31/76

I've never smelled flowers,
I've never seen trees.
I've never felt Levi's
rub on my knees.
I've never been happy
I never can smile.
I've never squished toothpaste
on blue bathroom tile.
But all that's a'changin',
and life will begin
The day I get out
of the U.S.N.

Birthdays

You would think that my brother would take one day off each year to stop harassing me, on my birthday, but this wasn't the case. He used this special day to create his own birthday cards with me typically being the moron character. Here's an example:

HERE'S THE EXTREMELY PROFESSIONAL SURFER, WAITING FOR THE WAVE OF THE DAY...

SUDDENLY... HE SPIES IT...
THUNDERING TOWARDS HIM
LIKE AN IMPENETRABLE
WALL OF WATER...

HE TURNS HIS BOARD...
HIS FACE SET WITH
HARD, DETERMINED LINES...
THE OTHER SURFERS
STARE LIKE GEEKS A'GAPIN'.

HE MOUNTS... CROUCHES...
WHEN SUDDENLY, FROM
BENEATH THE DEPTHS...

A GREAT NOISE ECHOS FROM BELOW, AND

DAVID!

Chapter 4

My Stupid Brother Gets His Own Chapter

Immaculate Deception

By Mike McNichols

I was eight years old when my brother arrived. I was uncertain about the origin of new human beings, so when my parents showed up with a scrawny, red, wrinkled thing they called "David," I was drawn closer to the mystery of reproduction. Babies, it seemed, were purchased at a store in the dark of night.

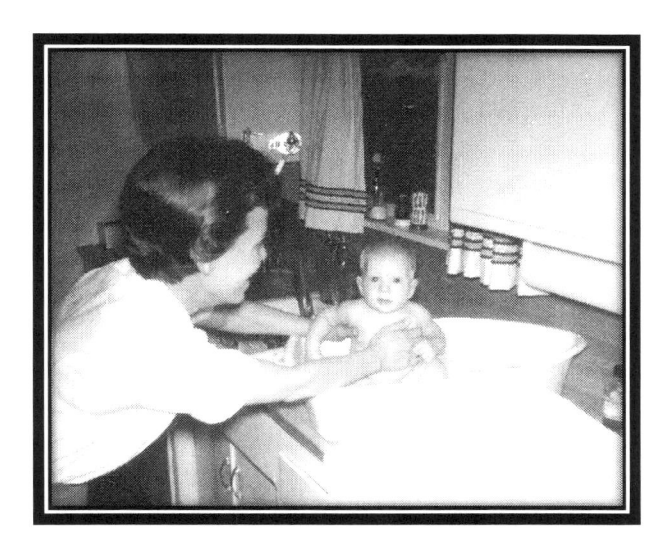

Having a new baby brother was a fun and interesting experience. I was clearly the big brother in this relationship and, as such, I was confident that I was special. Yes, my little brother had a specialness to him, but mine was an elder sibling specialness that was etched in history and would never, even upon my future death, be usurped by subsequent arrivals to our little family.

I was always glad to have David as my brother and, over time, our specialness became more of a shared thing than the claim to hierarchical power that I held as an eight-year-old. I came to understand that we were special in an egalitarian way, and by virtue of being obtained at retail establishments that trafficked in newborn infants, I outranked my brother only chronologically. I became quite comfortable with that arrangement.

Just a few months ago, as our 87-year-old mother was recuperating from an illness, she told me the back story of my brother's appearance in our family. She said that she had been content with having only one child (me), and since we were getting along fairly well, she had no plans to expand her cadre of children, especially since she was unable to give birth after I was born. My grandmother and great aunts decided this was a bit selfish of my mother and suggested that she consider adoption. She caved in to the pressure and mentioned the possibility to her doctor, who, in those ancient times, had the authority to arrange adoptions.

After a few months, Mom came home from shopping, and as she made her way through our house, she heard a voice in her head say, "I have a baby for you." The experience frightened her so badly that her knees gave out and she fell to the floor. She managed to stumble into her bedroom and sit on the edge of her bed, shaking like a trout on a line. As she attempted to recover, she heard the voice again: "I have a baby for you."

Mom said that she decided to make an appointment with the doctor and see if there was anything to this auditory visitation. She made a plan to approach the doctor in a nonchalant way, claiming that a small wart on her hand was in need of medical investigation. The day of the appointment came, and Mom sat in the examination room with the doctor, her wartish subterfuge in process.

She cleared her throat and tried to act casual. "So, did anything come about with that little adoption list that you had a while back?"

The doctor set down his instruments, sat back in his chair, and folded his arms. Fixing his eyes on Mom, he said, "I have a baby for you right now."

And the next thing you know, my brother came to live with us. This was a disturbing story to me because I had never in my whole life heard it before. So I interrogated my poor, sick mother.

"This really happened, Mom?"

"Yes, it really did."

"Why didn't you ever tell me this?"

"Oh, I told you this."

"Mom, I would have remembered this story. You never told me."

"I'm sure I did. It's no big deal."

"What do you mean 'it's no big deal'? Of course it's a big deal! God, or the universe, or some space alien tells you in your head that there's a baby for you and zippity-zip, there's Dave, and it's no big deal?" I was getting worked up.

"I know I told you."

"Does Dave know this story?"

"Sure he does. Would you get me a glass of water?"

My mother is good at changing the subject when things get out of her control.

I got Mom her water, said my see-you-laters, and headed home. On the way, I called my brother.

"Dave. Mom just told me the story of you being born, with the voice in the head and everything. Did you know about this?"

"Yup."

"Why did I not know this?" My egalitarian specialness was swirling around the drain of despair. "When did she tell you?"

"Last week."

"Last week. Really?"

"Really."

"You never heard this story in your entire life."

"Nope. Not until last week." He started laughing.

"Dave, if this is true, then it's absolutely amazing. I used to think I was the special one. Dude, you are now golden."

"Yes, I am, and now you suck."

"Indeed, I do."

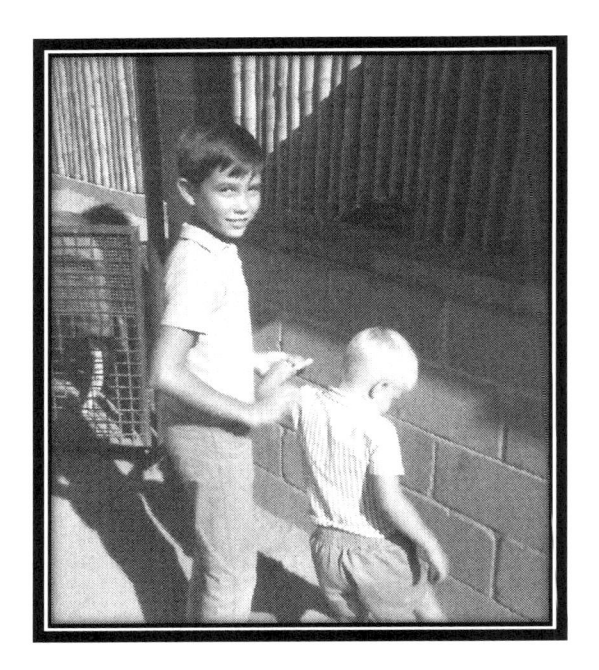

Chapter 5

My Lovely Wife

Dinner

Cindy didn't know how to prepare many meals when we got married; in fact she only knew one...lasagna. It was fantastic, but we couldn't eat it every night.

She learned how to make it from her nanny, who was born and raised in Sicily. It's the best I've ever had. After that, not so much. As a young married couple on a tight budget, working all day, we were looking for cheap and easy ideas for meals. She wanted to make a roast beef like my mom made. My mom would sear each side then slow roast it in a covered low-heat pan in water for hours. Then she would add potatoes and carrots for the last hour. Magnifico!

Cindy was looking for a similar idea without having to babysit it. We were given a Crock Pot as a wedding gift so her plan was to put a roast in the Crock Pot in water and cook it on low all day. By the time we would get home from work she could add potatoes and carrots, put it on high, and after 45 minutes or so...*wah lah*, dinner is served.

She goes to the grocery store to pick out a roast, and one catches her eye. There is a sticker on the package that reads, "Great for Crock Pot." Perfect! It's cheap too, about $1.50. She gets it with some veggies and heads home.

The next morning she puts it in the Crock Pot with some water, selects the low setting, and heads off to work. Quick, easy and cheap. She gets home before me and adds the potatoes and carrots. When I get home she splits the potatoes and carrots on our plates then puts the roast on a plate for us to share. We give thanks, and then I grab the knife and fork to cut our roast. Now, you need to imagine what it sounds like to run a serrated knife across the edge of a piece of steel. That's what it sounded like. I turned the plate around and tried the other side, thinking I was trying to cut on the bone side. Same thing. I tried everything I knew to find meat and couldn't. I sat there befuddled. Cindy got up and found the packaging in the trash. It was a stew bone. No meat. Hence, $1.50.

We laughed, I made fun of her, and then we went to McDonald's for dinner.

Sewing 101

I didn't take sewing in school. My mom knew how to sew and handled any sewing needs of mine while I was growing up. She did teach me how to sew on a button, but that was the extent of my sewing abilities. During the first year of our marriage I was working a job where I needed to wear long-sleeved dress shirts. One day at work I caught a sleeve on something, causing a small tear. I pointed it out to Cindy who said she could fix it. I told her that I could have my mom fix it, not realizing how dumb it was to say that. She told me that she was equipped and trained to fix it because she took home economics in high school. Whoop dee frickin do dah.

Home economics...a good idea. Teach kids how to run a house, make a meal, clean, wash clothes, sew, etc. I wonder if they still teach that today. I bet it has changed a little. They probably teach today's generation how to obtain a credit card, how to order a pizza, how to order a Caramel Macchiato, how to plug in a curling iron, flat iron, and hair dryer all in one outlet, how to get a tattoo, and how to stay informed by watching TMZ and reading *People* magazine...Nah...What am I thinking? Most kids know all this stuff by the time they're five years old.

Anyway, Cindy said she would fix it. She did and a couple days later I wore it to work. My job at this time was as a transportation supervisor on a freight dock at night. Lots of walking up and down the dock all night, fast-paced, directing and managing the flow of freight. As I was working that night I kept noticing that something in my shirt was irritating my arm. Like maybe she sewed it too tight, or the repair area was rubbing against my skin. I didn't have time to figure it out. It would bother me every few minutes and I would rub my arm and readjust my sleeve, then just move on.

Finally, late into my shift, I couldn't handle it anymore. I stopped and rolled up my sleeve to see what was causing this irritation. I found the needle still hooked to the thread hanging from the end of the 2-inch repair. Cindy must have missed the part about finishing the job. I should have had my mom fix it.

Facebook

Not only is this story something my wife did that is stupid, but it points out the stupidity of Facebook and people on Facebook. My wife spends a lot of time creating clever Facebook posts, and she prides herself on the amount of "likes" she gains. Don't we all? One evening she asks me to hand her her cell phone. I pick it up and inadvertently post a status for her on Facebook with my thumb. The status was "M." Within seconds people start to "like" it. Then our son comments, "3." Followed by someone commenting that his post was wrong, it should have been "N." He comments again, "3." The likes continue, and it grows to the most popular post of the year for her.

School Sports

One day during high school, Cindy is all suited up to run track. She stands on an outside basketball court and stretches. Then, while still looking down at her shoes, she starts to run, and runs directly into the steel pole that holds the basketball hoop. Many of her classmates saw her do this and remember it to this day.

Chapter 6

My Mother-In-Law

Nemo And Friends

Several years ago we took a family vacation to Disneyworld. Cindy and I along with two of our kids, Jason and Sara. We were joined by Cindy's younger sister Kim and her husband Kevin along with their three kids, Katie, Kristie, and Kevin. In addition, Cindy's Uncle Bill and her mom MaryAnn came along for the ride.

L-R: Kim Unland, Kevin Unland, Me, Sara McNichols, Katie Unland, Jason McNichols, Kevin Unland Jr (in front), Kristie Unland, Cindy McNichols, MaryAnn Freeland, Uncle Bill Freeland + two monsters

We stayed in some timeshare condos for a week and would join up at 9:00 each morning to devise a plan for the day. We visited each Disney Park throughout the week and would sometimes split our day to visit one park in the morning and another in the afternoon.

One day we were at Animal Kingdom, enjoying the various attractions, and a cast member approached our group inquiring about our visit, then proceeded to give us VIP passes to a show. Disney had a program at that time called "Year of a Million Dreams" and we were the lucky recipients of one of the gifts they offered. The show was called *Nemo and Friends*, a Broadway-type show based on the movie *Finding Nemo*. It was very exciting.

My mother-in-law, MaryAnn, had not been feeling well all day. She was suffering from diarrhea, which was a regular occurrence for her, and had been prescribed some medication to help stop it. The instructions were to take one pill every six hours as needed. She had taken some that morning but the meds weren't working so she was having a rough day.

In the midafternoon we arrive at the theater and are ushered to seats in the first two rows just off center stage right. Awesome seats. They fill up the theater with about 2,000 people and the show begins. Great costumes and scenery, great music, and a first-class production with us in the best seats in the house. About 15 minutes into the show some of the main characters are performing right in front of us, literally a few feet away. I notice that a couple of them look down near us, as if something is wrong.

Then I see my sister-in-law, Kim, step over the seat in front of us. MaryAnn has passed out cold right in front of me and is leaning on my nephew Kevin. Kim is a Captain with the LA County Sheriff's Department and is well experienced in helping those in need. She's trying to get her mom to wake up and asks me to call for help. I find a page and tell him to call 911, which he does.

Disney has personnel on staff that handle first aid and minor medical issues throughout the parks and they arrive quickly. In addition, an ambulance and paramedics have been summoned and are en route. Meanwhile the show continues while MaryAnn is half coming to and mostly still out of it. We're not sure what is wrong. Due to the commotion now happening in the front two rows, the show is suspended. A prerecorded message is played: "Ladies and gentlemen, *Nemo and Friends* is being temporarily delayed. Please remain seated and the show will continue in just a few moments." The house lights come up and everyone is staring at us and MaryAnn.

Maryann is starting to feel better at this point, and starts to sit and tell Kim that she's ok. Kim tells her that the show has been stopped and the whole theater is staring at them so she better just lie there and act sick. Next, I see the paramedics arrive and they are wheeling in a stretcher and some medical gear. They roll in the center aisle and prepare to come down the right side aisle to us. One of the paramedics grabs the handle of the large red toolbox that contains the meds and it is immediately apparent that the last person to use the box didn't close it properly because the box opens and all of the contents explode across the aisle. The paramedic closes his eyes and looks to the heavens in total disgust. 10 seconds later another announcement is made. "Ladies and gentlemen, today's performance of *Nemo and Friends* and has been cancelled. We are very sorry for this inconvenience. Please move towards the nearest exit. Thank you."

One of the paramedics attends to MaryAnn while the other retrieves all of the drugs, assisted by security. MaryAnn is still in and out of consciousness so they decide to take her to the hospital. They place her on the stretcher and wheel her backstage. Kim and I stay at her side. There's an ambulance ready backstage and they load her in the back. We decide to have Kim accompany MaryAnn and for me to drive Cindy and Uncle Bill to the hospital. The ambulance takes off while Cindy, Bill and I head for the car. The kids all stay with Kevin in the park.

It takes us a while to get through the exit and to our car, then about a 15-minute drive to the hospital. I pull in and drop off Cindy and Bill while I search for parking. Once parked, I head towards emergency and check in through security. I walk into the room where MaryAnn is and everyone is laughing: the doctor, Cindy, Bill, and Kim. MaryAnn was just rushed to the hospital in an ambulance, in and out of consciousness, and everyone is laughing. Hmmm. The doctor says that she overdosed on

Lomotil, which is an opioid. She was only supposed to take one every six hours but had doubled up and taken about five since breakfast. The doctor gave her something to counteract it and she would be fine. She was released within the hour and we were at dinner within a couple hours, all joking about her overdose.

The next Christmas I made a gift for MaryAnn to remind her of the Nemo experience. I bought a *Finding Nemo* children's book and changed the story to include MaryAnn's adventure: taking more than the recommended dose, it not working, taking more, getting front row seats, passing out, a fun ambulance ride to the hospital, then dinner at Chili's.

A couple years later we all took th~   ~ion to Disneyworld. On the day that we ᾿   ᾿ went to the theater and told a casᵢ given prime seating again, this tᵢ

MaryAnn Freeland

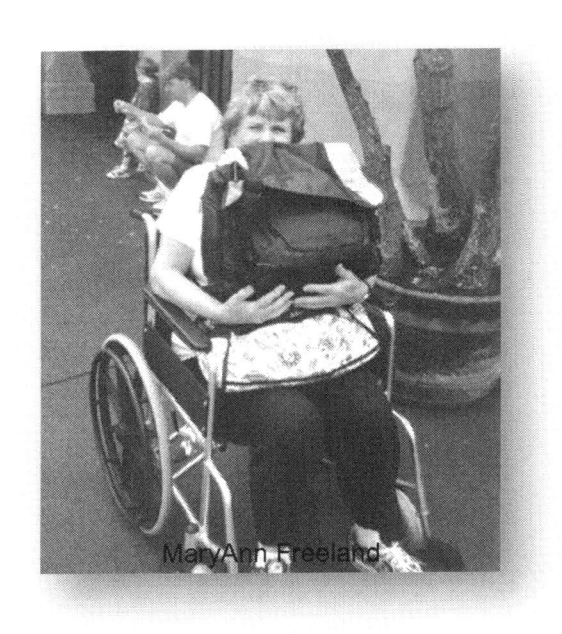

I'll Pay

My mother-in-law is very generous and always offers to pay her portion of any event or meal. On one of these many trips to Disneyworld the whole group converged upon a local Walmart after a long day of travel. It was late at night and the plan was to buy groceries for the week before heading to the condos.

MaryAnn, Uncle Bill, my sister-in-law Kim, her husband Kevin, and kids in tow all lined up at the check-out line with a ton of goods for breakfast, lunch, snacks, and drinks. MaryAnn was anxious to pay for the whole kit and caboodle, as she would say. She hurried up to the card reader and swiped her card before anyone else could. The only problem was that she had just paid for the gentleman in front of them. He wasn't done checking out yet. None the family's items had even been scanned yet.

The clerk couldn't figure out how to reverse her erroneous swipe, so they had to delete it. Then they took all of his goods, already in bags in a cart, and rescanned all of them while MaryAnn and crew waited.

Uncle Bill relayed this story to me since I wasn't there, as only he can, with utter disdain at having been delayed even longer into the night at a Walmart.

MaryAnn with Woody

Recycling

My mother-in-law is trying to do her part with the "Go Green" movement. She recycles. Cans, bottles, and even plastic Ziploc bags. Recently she joined her daughter Wendy and family on a vacation to Washington, D.C. She packed her shampoo, soap, and other items in a plastic Ziploc bag. She also made brownies for the trip and packed them in a Tupperware container, and placed these items in her suitcase.

During the first day in D.C., while visiting Lincoln Memorial, she offers some brownies to the family. Her grandsons, Ryan and Jonathan, take her up on the offer. As soon as they both take a bite they notice the strong taste and smell of soap. Turns out that MaryAnn recycled her soap-carrying Ziploc and turned it into a brownie-carrying Ziploc. Not all recycling is a good idea.

MaryAnn Freeland

L-R: Jonathan Schoeman, Uncle Bill Freeland, Ryan Schoeman

Birthday Party

My wife has two sisters: her twin sister, Wendy, and younger sister, Kim. When Cindy and Wendy were 10 years old, Kim was nine. Kim was invited to a birthday party of a schoolmate on a Saturday morning, so her mom dropped her off at what she thought was the home of the party, then rushed off for her busy Saturday schedule. Apparently MaryAnn was so busy that she didn't verify that Kim got into the house of the party before she drove off. It was the wrong house, and Kim had no idea where the right house was, so she just walked and eventually found her way home, about a mile away.

Kim Unland

Epilogue

So the fact that other people on the planet have done stupid things makes me feel better, because I'm not alone. Next, I need to understand why every driver on the road is an idiot, except me. Maybe that will be my next book.

Made in the USA
Lexington, KY
25 October 2019